The Best Casserole Cookbook Ever

THE *Best Casserole* COOKBOOK EVER

With More Than 500 Recipes!

○○○○○

by Beatrice Ojakangas
photographs by Susie Cushner

CHRONICLE BOOKS
SAN FRANCISCO

Library of Congress Cataloging-in-Publication Data available.

ISBN: 978-0-8118-5624-9

Manufactured in Canada

Designed by Katie Heit
Food Styling by Jee Levin
Prop Styling by Lynn Butler

10 9 8 7 6 5 4 3

Chronicle Books LLC
680 Second Street
San Francisco, California 94107

www.chroniclebooks.com

Dedicated to all lovers of casseroles and hot dishes.

ACKNOWLEDGMENTS

While writing this book, I likened the process to shoveling a six-foot snow bank with a teaspoon. Anyone who lives in Minnesota can identify with this. We have overdosed on casseroles, and more than one got buried in my walk-in cooler a bit too long. I started freezing them, and when the freezer filled up, I was grateful for friends who offered to help me retrieve the space.

I want to thank especially my husband, Dick, who was my ready tester, taster, and sometimes dishwasher, and who calls himself not just a "clean plate clubber," but also a "clean casserole clubber." Thanks also go to many friends and family members who contributed recipes and helped test and eat these recipes. I am, because of them, most blessed.

Thanks to Jane Dystel, my patient agent, who encouraged me to write this book, and Bill LeBlond, senior editor at Chronicle Books, who not only gave me the opportunity to write this book but believed that I could actually do it in a year.

Many thanks to Amy Treadwell, project editor at Chronicle Books, who gave me the choice of sending the book in either hard copy or electronically. When I chose the electronic option, Amy aptly answered, "The trees will thank you." And so it was that all six hundred–some pages amazingly flew across the country through the Internet. Thanks, too, to Deborah Kops for her excellent work in editing this monumental manuscript.

TABLE OF CONTENTS

INTRODUCTION

THE CASSEROLE IS BACK

Casseroles are making a comeback. They are all about home, food, family, and friends, whether you are cooking alone or together, no matter what season. Not only are casseroles fast and easy to make, but they can be healthy as well, with the addition of whole grains, legumes, and vegetables.

The word "casserole" can refer either to the dish that the food is cooked in or to the food itself. In Minnesota, however, the food is called a "hot dish." In other parts of the country, it might be called a "covered dish."

Casseroles became popular in the 1950s, mainly because they got the cook in and out of the kitchen fast. This was about the time that canned soups became vastly popular, and cooks were convinced that they, too, saved enormous amounts of time.

Today's casseroles have a greater variety of flavors, and they're fresher, too. We have embraced many dishes and ingredients from abroad, and we're also using more fresh vegetables, many of which are now available in convenient, ready-to-use packages. Ingredients like sun-dried tomatoes, brined olives, dried exotic mushrooms, flavored oils, and fresh herbs, which were not readily available in the past, are at our fingertips now.

In this book, there may be an occasional recipe here and there that uses a canned soup. However, my personal preference is to avoid ingredients that we've recently found to be unhealthy, such as monosodium glutamate (MSG), partially hydrogenated fats, and high-fructose corn syrup (a sweetener widely used in beverages and fruits). Read the labels.

It is my hope that you will find more than a few useful recipes in this book, as well as suggestions for those times when what to fix for a meal presents obstacles like (1) "I don't have time for fancy preparations," or (2) the opposite, "I really want to serve something special," or (3) "I want to serve something wonderful but I don't have the time," or (4) "I need to make it ahead and leave the baking for the final hour." Throughout this book there will be information to help you overcome these obstacles.

I love to entertain and usually have dreams of elegance and formality. But when it comes down to it, hospitality and conviviality are more important. As a result, we've had a lot of fun with our testing parties. When our guests took a recipe, made it, and offered suggestions, they invested themselves in the process, and proudly presented the results. This happened time and time again as we tested the recipes in this book.

CASSEROLE COOKWARE

○○○○○

A casserole dish itself can be made of ovenproof glass, porcelain, earthenware, or enameled cast iron. Glass, porcelain, and earthenware do not conduct heat quickly, but they do retain heat, so they are good choices for casseroles. Dishes made from one of these three materials can go from freezer to oven without problems, but they cannot be used for stove-top cooking like cast-iron or enameled cast-iron casseroles can. Most casseroles are attractive enough to go from oven to table.

In some of the recipes, we specify the size of a casserole dish in quarts, rather than giving its dimensions. This is because if you know the volume, you can use a casserole or baking dish with a different shape and dimensions. I have casserole dishes that are round, oval, square, rectangular, and even star-shaped. Any of them would work for most casseroles that call for a shallow casserole dish of a certain volume. To determine the volume of an odd-shaped dish, you can simply measure it using quarts of water. If there is no size indicated on the bottom of a dish, I mark it with a permanent marker. Ovenproof dishes that have the size on the bottom, like a 9-by-13-inch baking dish, often include the volume. Dish dimensions do make a difference in baking time. If the depth of the dish, and therefore the food, is greater, it will need to bake longer than it would in a shallow dish. Some casseroles fare best when they are baked in a deep casserole dish with a cover. The recipes indicate when this type of dish is needed.

FREEZING & THAWING BAKED CASSEROLES

○○○○○

To successfully freeze foods, there are some simple rules you need to follow. The two most important bits of advice are to make sure you wrap the foods very well and to keep track of what is in your freezer. Freezer burn happens when food becomes dehydrated as a result of improper packing and being held too long.

To freeze casseroles:
Cool completely after baking and cover with plastic wrap or waxed paper, and then with foil. Label the dish with its name, date of preparation, number of servings, and hints on how to reheat the food.

To thaw frozen casseroles:
Remove from the freezer at least 8 hours ahead or defrost overnight in the refrigerator, then reheat in the oven to serving temperature. In a pinch, you can thaw a casserole in the microwave, but be sure it is in a microwave-safe container. Microwaves tend to thaw foods from the outside in. The center may still be frozen while the outside is burning. To avoid this, use a low setting and turn the food often.

ASSEMBLING & REFRIGERATING CASSEROLES BEFORE BAKING

○○○○○

Many of the recipes that follow can be assembled, covered, and refrigerated for several hours, or even a day. If you have chilled a casserole for more than a few hours, remove it from the refrigerator when you preheat the oven. That will give the ingredients and the dish a chance to warm up a bit.

HOSTING A POTLUCK

○○○○○

Casseroles can be shared with pride. "Can I bring something?" These are words we often hear when we invite friends or family to a party. The idea seems so American, but it is actually done the world over.

Although the term "potluck" suggests a random assortment of dishes, it's likely to turn out better if the host does a little bit of organizing. The term itself has an old-fashioned ring to it. We might visualize ladies in their Sunday bonnets, teetering on high heels, carrying large dishes covered with checkered cloths. But potluck parties are an ideal form of entertaining for the contemporary host or hostess who would like to gather friends together, but who is too busy to do all of the cooking.

If you are organizing a potluck, you can make a point of asking each person to bring a favorite dish. If you can, be more specific—for example, "Your special turkey-and-stuffing casserole would be perfect," or "Can you bring your wonderful vegetable casserole?" The more than 500 recipes in this book are all great choices for a potluck, and most of them are very portable, requiring no elaborate last-minute preparation.

A potluck with a theme can be a lot of fun for a group of

friends. Themes like Italian, French, Scandinavian, German, or South American can pique everyone's imagination. I know of families who, for their annual holiday gatherings, ask people to bring foods that start with the letter "C" or "H" or that are a certain color.

If you choose to organize your potluck, here are some more ideas. (1) ask guests to bring a family favorite dish; or (2) assign each guest to bring either an appetizer, main dish, or dessert; or (3) as the host, you can provide the main dish and ask the guests to bring appetizers and side dishes.

When assigning dishes, be considerate of guests who are traveling a long distance, and recommend they bring non-perishables, such as cookies, bread, or pickles. If you have oven space, suggest a ready-to-bake casserole that can be kept cold until they arrive. At the party, it is always helpful to label dishes. I use 3-inch white ceramic tiles, purchased on sale from a hardware store, and write with a felt-tip pen the names of various dishes. The tiles are easily washed clean for use another time.

It is the host's responsibility to provide serving utensils, pot holders, dishes, and silverware. It's also nice to have small disposable containers for leftovers and cards for sharing recipes (ask guests to bring recipes). Be sure to have plenty of spatulas and big spoons for serving.

Put beverages into a large container, such as a barrel, tub, or planter, with ice to keep them cold. Be sure to have nonalcoholic beverages available.

If you have a large number of guests, set out small platters of food and replenish them as needed. When replenishing perishable food, replace or wash the platter first to prevent contamination.

To prevent guests from "double dipping" with their eating utensils, put a spoon in each dip or spread so they can drop a small amount on their plates.

Provide adequate places for people to dispose of garbage and deposit used dishes. Keep garbage away from food that will be served. Don't mix dirty and clean dishes.

KEEPING FOOD SAFE

○○○○○

Keep hot foods hot (above 145°F) and cold foods cold (below 45°F) to avoid bacterial growth. Never leave foods at room temperature for more than 2 hours. It is not a good idea to let food sit out all afternoon. Instead, designate the time of serving and keep it to less than 2 hours before; refrigerate leftovers immediately.

TOOLS FOR YOUR KITCHEN

○○○○○

You don't need a lot of tools, but there are some that make life much easier for the cook.

KNIVES AND HAND TOOLS

- 8- to 10-inch chef's knife for cutting and chopping
- Serrated knife for slicing breads, tomatoes, and soft fruit

- Paring knife
- Potato peeler
- Can opener
- Box grater
- Zester or Microplane for removing zest from citrus fruits
- Wooden spoons for cooking
- Large metal spoons, some of them slotted, for serving
- Whisk
- Tongs
- Rubber spatulas

CUTTING BOARDS

- Two boards, one designated for raw meat and fish, to prevent cross-contamination. The new thin, plastic cutting sheets are handy, and they come two or three in a pack. (Never cut cooked meat on the same board on which it was cut before cooking.)

MEASURING TOOLS

- Set of measuring spoons. It usually includes tablespoon, teaspoon, ½ teaspoon, and ¼ teaspoon measures; some sets include ½ tablespoon and ⅛ teaspoon measures, too.
- Set of dry cup measures. It usually includes 1 cup, ½ cup, ⅓ cup, and ¼ cup measures. (Dry measures are always used to measure the dry ingredients by leveling with the top of the cup.)
- Liquid measuring cups. These have markings for fractions of a cup. It is handy to have both 1-cup and a 2-cup measures.

BOWLS

- Set of nested glass bowls. These are great because glass can be used in the microwave.
- Set of metal bowls, usually three or four bowls that nest together.

POTS AND PANS

- Medium saucepan with a lid
- Small nonstick skillet
- Medium or large skillet with a lid
- Medium or large Dutch oven
- Large pot for pasta
- Roasting pan with a rack, which can double as a lasagna pan

CASSEROLES

(glass, porcelain, or enameled cast iron)

- 2- to 4-cup for appetizers
- 1-quart for small dishes, 6- or 8-quart for larger dishes, and one or two sizes in between
- Shallow casseroles in oval, rectangular, square, and novelty shapes
- Deep, heavy casseroles (or a Dutch oven) with lids
- 9-by-13-inch baking dish

- And, of course, good hot pads!

Chapter 1
CASSEROLE BASICS

The whole idea of this chapter—in fact, the idea behind this whole book—is to offer healthier, tastier casserole choices. One simple way to accomplish this is to make your own sauces to replace the "cream of" soups. Of course, if you don't really care, you can go ahead and use canned soups.

Here's my rationale for making your own sauce: While "cream of" soups offer convenience, they are high in sodium. Just read the labels. You'll also notice MSG (monosodium glutamate), partially hydrogenated fat or oil (a source of trans fats), and various chemical flavor enhancers.

Each of the basic sauce recipes here replaces one can (10¾ ounces) of concentrated soup. You can use them in your favorite casserole recipes. If the casserole recipe calls for 2 cans, just double the sauce recipe. You will have less sodium and fewer unknowns in your food, which ultimately gives you more control over what you are feeding yourself and your family.

If you use purchased broths, select the low-sodium varieties. I look for organic broths that are low in salt. If you would like to make your own, you will find simple recipes for making three kinds of broth: chicken (page 25), beef (page 26), and vegetable (page 27). Again, making your own gives you more control over what you are eating.

BASIC MIX 'N' MATCH MEAL-IN-ONE-CASSEROLE RECIPE

Casseroles are basically a combination of meat, pasta, rice, beans, or veggies with a sauce and perhaps a topping, baked in the oven until bubbly. A friend once described a casserole as a blend of inspiration and what's on hand. Certain elements are important for a one-dish meal or, as we say in Minnesota, a "hot dish." To inspire you to be creative (or help you clean out the refrigerator), here is a basic plan.

SERVES 6

FOR THE PROTEIN
(SELECT 1 OR COMBINE A FEW TO EQUAL 2 CUPS):

Chopped hard-cooked egg

Diced cooked chicken or turkey

Diced cooked ham

Cooked ground beef

Cooked beef or pork, shredded or cubed

Cooked fish, flaked

Cooked shelled shrimp

Cooked dry beans, peas, or other legumes

FOR THE STARCH
(SELECT 1 OR MORE TO EQUAL 3 CUPS COOKED):

Pasta in fancy shapes, shells, or tubes, such as penne or elbow macaroni

Wide or narrow egg noodles, or strands of pasta, such as spaghetti or linguine

Long- or short-grain brown or white rice or wild rice

FOR THE VEGETABLE
(SELECT 1 OR MORE TO EQUAL 2 CUPS COOKED):

Broccoli florets

Green beans, trimmed and cut into ½-inch pieces

Peas

Zucchini, sliced, diced, or chopped

Sautéed chopped or sliced onion and/or sliced mushrooms

FOR THE SAUCE
(SELECT 1 TO MEASURE 1¼ TO 2 CUPS):

Basic White Sauce (page 18), or 1 can (10 ¾ ounces) condensed cream of mushroom, celery, or a similar soup

Basic Egg Sauce (page 19), or 1 can condensed cream of mushroom, celery, or a similar soup

Basic Cheese Sauce (page 20), or 1 can condensed cream of mushroom, celery, or a similar soup

Basic Mushroom Sauce (page 22), or 1 can condensed cream of mushroom, celery, or a similar soup

Sour cream or mayonnaise

Whole, stewed, or diced tomatoes, with juice

FOR THE FLAVOR INGREDIENTS
(SELECT 1 OR MORE TO EQUAL ¼ TO ½ CUP):

Chopped celery

Chopped onion

Sliced black olives

FOR THE HERBS
(SELECT 1 OR MORE, 1 TEASPOON DRIED TO 3 TABLESPOONS FRESH):

Mixed dried or chopped fresh herbs, such as basil, thyme, marjoram, and rosemary

FOR THE TOPPING
(SELECT 1 OR MORE TO EQUAL ¼ TO ½ CUP):

Grated or shredded cheese, such as Swiss, Cheddar, Monterey Jack, or Parmesan

Buttered breadcrumbs

1. Preheat the oven to 350°F. Lightly butter a 2½- to 3-quart casserole.

2. Select and prepare the ingredients of your choice from each of the categories listed above.

3. Mix the protein, starch, and vegetables in a large bowl. In a smaller bowl, mix the sauce, flavor ingredients, and herbs. Spread the starch mixture in the bottom of the casserole and pour the sauce over the top. Sprinkle with the topping.

4. Bake, covered, for 30 minutes. Uncover and bake for another 15 minutes, or until heated through.

BASIC WHITE SAUCE

This thick white sauce is a basic replacement for a can of "cream of" soup, and you can use it in your favorite casserole recipe. To make a sauce to replace cream of chicken soup, substitute chicken broth for the milk. To replace cream of mushroom soup, sauté ½ pound sliced mushrooms in the butter before adding the flour and substitute beef broth for the hot milk. Add any seasonings according to your taste.

MAKES 1¼ CUPS;
REPLACES 1 CAN (10¾ OUNCES) CONDENSED SOUP

- 4 tablespoons butter
- ¼ cup all-purpose flour
- ½ teaspoon salt
- ¼ teaspoon pepper
- 1 cup hot milk

1. In a medium saucepan, melt the butter. Stir in the flour, salt, and pepper and cook over medium heat, stirring constantly, for 3 minutes, or until the mixture is smooth and bubbly.

2. Whisk in the hot milk, keeping the mixture smooth and free of lumps. Bring to a boil, whisking constantly, reduce the heat, and cook until thickened and smooth. Use the sauce hot, or cover and refrigerate until ready to use.

BASIC EGG SAUCE

Use this mixture, which does not require any stove-top cooking, when you don't want to make Basic White Sauce (facing page). Use it to replace 1 can of "cream of" soup. The proportions are easy to remember: Just add 2 eggs to 1 cup milk and season to your taste. To use as a replacement for cream of chicken soup, substitute chicken broth for the milk.

MAKES 1¼ CUPS;
REPLACES 1 CAN (10¾ OUNCES) CONDENSED SOUP

1 cup milk

2 large eggs

½ teaspoon salt

¼ teaspoon pepper

Mix together the milk, eggs, salt, and pepper in a medium bowl. Pour over any unbaked casserole that requires 1 can (10¾ ounces) of condensed soup.

BASIC CHEESE SAUCE

This easy-to-make sauce is a great binder for casseroles, and it can also be spooned over cooked cauliflower or broccoli, poached eggs, chicken breasts, or even fish.

MAKES 2½ CUPS;
REPLACES 2 CANS (10¾ OUNCES EACH) CONDENSED SOUP

4 tablespoons butter

¼ cup all-purpose flour

½ teaspoon salt

1 pinch cayenne pepper

⅛ teaspoon dry mustard

2 cups hot milk

1 cup shredded Cheddar cheese

1. In a medium saucepan, melt the butter. Stir in the flour, salt, cayenne, and dry mustard until blended.

2. Whisk in the hot milk, bring to a boil, lower the heat, and cook, whisking constantly, until thickened and smooth. Add the cheese and stir until smooth. Use the sauce hot, or cover and refrigerate until ready to use.

BÉCHAMEL SAUCE

Béchamel sauce, or French white sauce, is often used in creamed dishes and casseroles. In the '50s, the sauce began to be replaced in everyday cooking by a cream soup of one sort or another. Made from scratch, this sauce will provide a fresher flavor for your dishes.

MAKES ABOUT 2¼ CUPS SAUCE;
REPLACES 2 CANS (10¾ OUNCES EACH) CONDENSED SOUP

4 tablespoons (½ stick) butter

¼ cup all-purpose flour

1 cup homemade (page 25) or prepared chicken broth, heated

½ cup cream or undiluted evaporated milk, heated

Salt

Dash of nutmeg

1. In a saucepan over medium heat, melt the butter, add the flour, and cook together for 2 to 3 minutes to remove the flour's raw taste.

2. Whisk in the heated broth and cream, stirring constantly, and cook until smooth and thick. Season with salt to taste and nutmeg. Use the sauce hot, or cover and refrigerate until ready to use.

BASIC MUSHROOM SAUCE

Mushroom sauce made with fresh mushrooms and beef broth makes a flavorful alternative to cream of mushroom soup. Use it in your favorite casserole recipe. For a richer and deeper flavor, instead of common white button mushrooms, use wild mushrooms such as morels or chanterelles, or shiitake or cremini mushrooms.

MAKES 1¾ CUPS;
REPLACES 1 CAN (10¾ OUNCES) CONDENSED SOUP

4 tablespoons butter

½ pound mushrooms, finely chopped

¼ cup onions, finely diced

¼ cup all-purpose flour

½ teaspoon salt

⅛ teaspoon pepper

1 cup homemade (page 26) or prepared beef broth, heated

1. In a medium saucepan, melt the butter over medium heat. Add the mushrooms and onions and sauté until aromatic. Add the flour, salt, and pepper, stirring until the mushrooms and onions are thoroughly coated.

2. Gradually add the beef broth and stir until the sauce is thickened, about 3 to 5 minutes. Use the sauce hot, or cover and refrigerate until ready to use.

SAVORY TOMATO SAUCE

When tomatoes are not in season, canned tomatoes are best. Use this sauce with cooked pasta or whenever a recipe calls for tomato sauce.

MAKES 3 CUPS

2½ cups peeled vine-ripened tomatoes or canned tomatoes, chopped (see Note)

3 tablespoons butter

1 medium onion, minced

3 tablespoons all-purpose flour

½ teaspoon dried thyme

Salt

Pepper

1. Whirl the tomatoes in a food processor or blender to puree.

2. In a 2-quart heavy saucepan, melt the butter over medium heat. Add the onion and cook for 3 to 5 minutes, until the onion is soft. Blend in the flour and stir over medium heat for 2 minutes, stirring until the onion is coated with flour.

3. Gradually add the pureed tomatoes to the onion mixture, stirring constantly. Cook, stirring, until thickened and smooth. Add the thyme and salt and pepper to taste. Use the sauce hot, or cover and refrigerate until ready to use.

○○○○○

NOTE: Fresh, vine-ripened tomatoes in season have great flavor. The rest of the year, however, the tomatoes from the supermarket are relatively tasteless. In most cases, canned tomatoes can be substituted in casseroles. Since they are usually picked at the height of the season, they actually have more flavor than those pale, out-of-season fresh tomatoes.

QUICK ALFREDO SAUCE

Alfredo sauce is credited to Chef Alfredo di Lello, who combined it with cooked fettuccine in the early 1900s. Since then, we've found many ways to use this sauce and even make changes in its preparation. In this simple-to-make version, cream cheese replaces the cream in the original sauce.

MAKES ABOUT 2¾ CUPS

1 package (8 ounces) cream cheese

1 cup milk

4 tablespoons butter

1 cup grated Parmesan cheese

1. Combine all of the ingredients in a medium saucepan and place over low heat.

2. Heat until the ingredients are melted and well combined, stirring frequently, approximately 15 minutes. Use in a casserole or simply pour over the pasta of your choice. Use the sauce hot, or cover and refrigerate until ready to use.

BASIC CHICKEN BROTH

The best thing about making your own chicken broth is that you decide what goes in it, and you can vary the flavors, too. For instance, you can add fresh herbs, more or less onion, and even garlic, if you prefer. A concentrated chicken broth is easy to make by simply boiling down the final product until it is thick or syrupy. Store it in the freezer in measured amounts, such as 1 or 2 cups, and use as needed.

MAKES 2 QUARTS

3 pounds chicken bones, or 1 whole stewing hen, rinsed and cut up

1 large onion, quartered

1 carrot (leave skin on), cut into 1-inch chunks

1 rib celery, cut into 1-inch chunks

2 sprigs fresh parsley

1 bay leaf

1 sprig fresh thyme, or ½ teaspoon dried thyme

3 quarts cold water

1 teaspoon salt, plus more to taste

1 teaspoon pepper, plus more to taste

1. Put all of the ingredients in a large stockpot and bring to a boil over high heat. Reduce the heat to low and simmer, partially covered, for 2 to 3 hours, or until the chicken is falling off the bones (if you have used a stewing hen). Check the stock every 30 minutes and skim off and discard any foam that rises to the surface.

2. Strain the broth. If you have used a hen, pick large pieces of meat off the bones and reserve for making soup. Discard the bones and vegetables.

3. Season the broth with more salt and pepper to taste. Cool and refrigerate until the fat has congealed. Remove the solid fat from the top of the broth and discard.

4. To store, measure the broth into heavy-duty resealable plastic bags, label, and freeze.

BASIC BEEF BROTH

For a deep, rich broth, roast the bones and vegetables before proceeding to step 2. A long, slow simmer of at least 3 hours is essential for a flavorful broth. For a clearer one, avoid boiling.

MAKES 3½ QUARTS

3 to 4 pounds meaty beef bones, such as short ribs or shank, tail, and/or neck bones

1 large onion (leave skin on), roughly chopped (see Note)

3 large carrots (leave skin on), roughly chopped

3 stalks celery, including leaves, roughly chopped

1 large tomato, chopped

8 whole black peppercorns

4 sprigs fresh parsley

1 bay leaf

1 tablespoon salt

2 teaspoons dried thyme

2 cloves garlic (optional)

4 quarts water

1. Preheat the oven to 450°F, and roast the bones and vegetables for about 30 minutes, if desired.

2. Combine all of the ingredients in a large stockpot. Bring the mixture to a boil and immediately reduce the heat. Simmer, partially covered, for 3 hours, or until the meat is falling off the bones. Check the stock every 30 minutes and skim and discard any foam that rises to the top of the pot.

3. Strain the broth well, pressing down on the meat and vegetables to extract their juices. Discard the meat, bones, and vegetables.

4. Cool and refrigerate until the fat has congealed. Remove the solid fat from top of the broth and discard. Taste and add seasonings as desired.

5. To store, measure the broth into heavy-duty resealable plastic bags, label, and freeze.

○○○○○

NOTE: The onion skin will add color to the broth.

BASIC VEGETABLE BROTH

Vegetable broth is perfect for vegetarian dishes. If you wish, collect the ingredients in resealable plastic bags and freeze until you have time to make this flavorful broth. To further concentrate the flavor, simmer the finished broth until it is reduced to 4 cups. Add water, cream, or milk to thin it when you use it in a sauce.

MAKES 2½ QUARTS

1 tablespoon olive oil

2 cups potato peels from scrubbed potatoes

1 large onion (leave skin on), coarsely chopped (see Note, facing page)

1 cup coarsely chopped mushrooms

2 stalks celery, including leaves, coarsely chopped

2 large carrots (leave skin on), coarsely chopped

1 bunch green onions (white and green parts), coarsely chopped

6 to 8 large cloves garlic, chopped

1 bunch fresh parsley

6 sprigs fresh thyme

2 bay leaves

1 teaspoon salt

3 quarts water

1. In a large stockpot, heat the olive oil over medium-high heat. Add the potato peels, onion, mushrooms, celery, carrots, green onions, and garlic cloves. Cook, stirring frequently, for 10 minutes.

2. Add the parsley, thyme, bay leaves, salt, and water and bring to a boil. Lower the heat and simmer, uncovered, for 1 hour and 30 minutes.

3. Strain the broth and discard the vegetables. Cool the broth. Refrigerate or measure into resealable freezer bags and freeze until ready to use.

BASIC COOKED RICE

Many recipes suggest that you "serve over hot fluffy rice." Here is a basic recipe that will provide four ½-cup servings.

MAKES 2 CUPS COOKED RICE

1¾ cups water

¾ teaspoon salt

1 tablespoon butter or olive oil (optional)

1 cup white or brown rice

1. In a medium saucepan, bring the water, salt, and butter or oil (if using) to a boil over high heat.

2. Stir in the rice slowly, so as not to disturb the boiling.

3. Cover, reduce the heat, and simmer for 20 to 30 minutes for white rice, or 35 to 45 minutes for brown rice.

4. Fluff the rice with a fork.

COOKED WILD RICE

Perfectly cooked wild rice is tender, but not entirely opened up. When wild rice is overcooked, it almost explodes into curly, white grains and gets mushy. Wild rice is the seed of a wild grass. It complements all sorts of main courses, from beef to fish. I seldom mix it with another type of rice because the cooking times will vary. In fact, the cooking time may vary from one package of wild rice to the next, depending on how the rice was processed, meaning how much the grain has been dried.

MAKES 2 CUPS

⅔ cup wild rice

2½ cups water

½ to 1 teaspoon salt

1. Put the rice into a strainer and run hot tap water over it until the water runs clear. This will remove any dust and foreign particles.

2. Bring the water and salt to a boil in a medium, heavy saucepan and add the wild rice. Stir, cover, and lower the heat. Simmer the rice for 30 to 40 minutes, without stirring, until tender.

3. Drain the excess water from the rice. It should be tender but not curled or mushy. Some kernels will be open, but others will be just tender.

COOKED DRIED BEANS

You can use this recipe to cook any variety of beans. If time is short, use the "quick soak" method, but if possible, soak the beans overnight. Extra cooked beans can be frozen for later use.

MAKES 6 TO 8 CUPS COOKED BEANS

1 pound dried beans (about 2 cups)

Quick method: Rinse and sort the beans in a large pot and add 6 to 8 cups hot water, covering the beans by at least 2 inches. Bring to a rapid boil for 2 minutes. Remove from the heat. Cover and let stand for 1 hour. Drain and rinse the beans and put them back in the pot. Add hot water to cover the beans by 2 inches, bring to a simmer, and simmer gently, with the lid tilted slightly, until the beans are tender, about 1½ to 2 hours.

Overnight method: Rinse and sort the beans in a large pot. Add 6 to 8 cups cold water or enough to cover the beans by 2 inches. Let stand overnight for at least 6 to 8 hours. Drain and rinse the beans. Put them back in the pot and add 6 cups hot water or enough to cover the beans by 2 inches. Simmer gently, with the lid tilted slightly, until the beans are tender, about 1½ to 2 hours.

To make it easy to use the beans, cool them completely, separate into 2-cup batches, and freeze in plastic bags for later use.

CARAMELIZED ONIONS

Caramelized onions are delicious baked over chicken breasts (see Chicken Breasts with Caramelized Onions on page 501). They are also delicious on grilled hamburgers and open-faced sandwiches. This is one of my favorite ways to prepare them. A bit of brown sugar gives the onions a start on sweetness. Some cooks like to make a heaping skillet full of onions. They cook down as they brown. If you make these ahead of time so they're ready to use, pack them in freezer bags or containers, marked with the date and amount.

MAKES ABOUT 2 CUPS

2 tablespoons butter

2 large sweet onions (about 2 pounds), thinly sliced

2 teaspoons packed light brown sugar

1. Melt the butter in a large skillet; add the onions and cook over medium-high heat for 10 minutes, or until well browned. Reduce the heat to medium and cook for another 30 minutes, or until soft, stirring frequently.

2. Add the brown sugar and stir until dissolved. Keep warm until ready to use. Or transfer to a covered container and refrigerate for up to 2 days or freeze up to 4 weeks.

FLAKY PASTRY

Including lemon juice and egg in the dough is an old-fashioned trick for making a flaky pastry. Use this recipe for pies with savory or sweet fillings. For a double-crust pie, double all of the ingredients except the egg; replace the egg yolk with 1 whole large egg.

MAKES ONE 8- OR 9-INCH PIECRUST

¾ cup all-purpose flour

¼ teaspoon salt

5 tablespoons chilled butter or lard

1 large egg yolk

1 teaspoon fresh lemon juice

2 to 4 tablespoons ice water

1. In a large bowl, combine the flour and salt. Using a pastry blender, two knives, or a pastry fork, cut in the butter or lard until the fat is the size of dried peas. Alternatively, combine the ingredients in a food processor with the steel blade in place, and pulse.

2. In a small bowl, whisk together the egg yolk, lemon juice, and 2 to 3 tablespoons of the ice water. Drizzle the egg mixture over the flour mixture. With a fork or spatula, mix until the pastry holds together in a ball, adding more ice water if necessary.

3. Turn out onto a work surface and knead lightly once or twice to shape the dough into a ball. Wrap in aluminum foil or plastic wrap and refrigerate until firm, about 30 minutes, before rolling out the dough. Proceed as directed in the recipe you are using.

Variation

Whole-Wheat Pastry: Substitute ¾ cup whole-wheat flour for ¾ cup of the all-purpose flour in the recipe.

FOOLPROOF HARD-COOKED EGGS

Here's how to cook eggs and avoid the green ring around the yolk.

Large eggs

1. Put the eggs into a pot, and cover with cold water by 1 to 2 inches. Place over high heat and bring to a boil, then remove from the heat. Cover, and let the eggs sit in the hot water for exactly 15 minutes.

2. Place the eggs, still in the pan, under cold running water and continue running the water over the eggs until the water in the pan is cold. These eggs will be easy to shell if you do it immediately.

NOTES: To make chilled eggs easier to shell, bring some water to a boil in a saucepan. Plunge the eggs in the boiling water for 10 seconds, remove, and put them in ice water.

To shell the eggs, tap them on the countertop to crack the shells all over. Remove the shells, beginning at the flatter end of the egg.

TACO SEASONING MIX

One good reason to make your own taco seasoning mix is that you can control what is in it. If you wish, you can make it less spicy by reducing the cayenne pepper or more spicy by adding more.

MAKES ABOUT 1¼ CUPS

2 tablespoons onion powder

2 tablespoons chili powder

2 teaspoons paprika

1 teaspoon cayenne pepper

1½ teaspoons dried oregano leaves

½ teaspoon dried marjoram leaves

1 tablespoon salt

¼ teaspoon black pepper

2 tablespoons cornstarch

1 tablespoon minced garlic

1 teaspoon ground cumin

Combine all of the ingredients in a small bowl and blend well. Store at room temperature in a tightly closed container, such as a canning jar or plastic container. Use within 6 months.

ROASTED PEPPERS

Several recipes call for roasted peppers. You can roast any type of bell pepper as well as large chile peppers, such as anchos or poblanos. Roast the peppers in the oven or over a gas range or grill.

Bell peppers or large chile peppers

Olive oil or vegetable oil

1. Preheat the oven to 500 to 550°F and cover a baking sheet with aluminum foil. Or prepare a very hot fire in a charcoal grill. Or turn the gas burner and hood fan on high.

2. Coat the peppers lightly with oil (if roasting on a gas burner, do not oil the peppers). Roast on the baking sheet in the oven or on the grill or burner. As the peppers develop charred spots, turn them over using a pair of long tongs. Continue roasting until the peppers are charred all over, about 15 minutes in the oven or 10 to 15 minutes on the grill.

3. Put the peppers in a paper bag or wrap in the foil used to cover the baking sheet. Allow to steam and cool for 10 to 15 minutes. Remove the stems and seeds and pull off the thin skins.

Chapter 2

CASSEROLE APPETIZERS & FIRST COURSES

Many of the recipes in this chapter serve a large number of people. When we serve appetizers, it's often for a party or a potluck, where we want to serve a bigger crowd. The advantage of casserole appetizers is that most of them can be assembled ahead, covered, and refrigerated, to be baked just before serving. This makes them easy to bring to a party—providing you let the host or hostess know your dish will need a few minutes in the oven. If you bake just before you leave your kitchen, be sure to keep the dish hot in an insulated tote bag.

The recipes are organized here by numbers of servings, starting with smaller yields.

BUTTERY PORTOBELLO MUSHROOMS WITH FRIED SAGE LEAVES

The flavors of butter-fried sage, lemon, and portobello mushrooms make this an outstanding first course. It's easiest to serve the mushrooms whole for a sit-down meal. For a "walk around" party, I like to cut the mushrooms into squares and serve with toothpicks.

SERVES 4

4 large portobello mushrooms (see Note)

4 tablespoons butter

¼ cup olive oil

5 bunches fresh sage leaves (about 40 leaves)

Salt

Pepper

1 lemon, halved

1. Preheat the oven to 400°F.

2. Trim the stems off the mushrooms and save for another use or discard. Arrange the mushrooms, gill sides up, in a shallow casserole.

3. In a small skillet, heat the butter and olive oil until bubbly. Add the sage leaves and cook over medium heat until the leaves are crispy.

4. Arrange the sage leaves on the mushrooms and drizzle the caps with the butter and olive oil mixture. Sprinkle with salt and pepper to taste.

5. Bake, uncovered, for 10 minutes, or until the mushrooms are tender. Squeeze the lemon over the mushrooms and serve.

○○○○○

NOTE: For serving buffet-style, cut the mushrooms into 1-inch squares before you put them in the casserole. Serve with sliced bread, or offer toothpicks for spearing.

SPICY CHEESE AND GREEN CHILE DIP

Serve this dip with raw veggies, crisp tortilla chips, or sliced crusty bread.

SERVES 6

1 can (14½ ounces) stewed tomatoes, drained

1 medium red onion, cut into 1-inch chunks

¼ cup packed chopped fresh parsley

1 can (4 ounces) diced green chiles with their juice

1 medium clove garlic

1 tablespoon white wine vinegar

1 teaspoon dried oregano

½ teaspoon salt

2 cups shredded Monterey Jack cheese, divided

1. Preheat the oven to 375°F. Coat a 1-quart ovenproof crock or casserole with cooking spray.

2. Put the drained tomatoes, onion, parsley, chiles, garlic, vinegar, oregano, and salt in a food processor with the steel blade in place. (Alternatively, you might use a blender, but be careful not to overprocess the mixture.) Process the mixture until the tomatoes and onions are coarsely chopped. Transfer to the casserole, stir in ½ cup of the shredded cheese, then top with the remaining 1½ cups cheese. (At this point you can cover and refrigerate the dish and heat it just before serving.)

3. Bake, uncovered, for 20 minutes or until the dip is hot and the cheese is melted. Serve hot.

CREAMY CRAB SPREAD WITH ALMONDS

Assemble this appetizer ahead of time and store it in the refrigerator. It's a perfect one to take to a potluck and heat when you arrive.

SERVES 6

Butter for the dish

1 package (8 ounces) cream cheese, softened (see Note)

2 cans or packages (6 ounces each) crabmeat, picked through

1 small onion, chopped

Pinch of cayenne pepper

⅓ cup sliced almonds

Crackers or melba toast for serving

1. Preheat the oven to 350°F. Butter a small 3-cup casserole.

2. In a small bowl, mix the cream cheese, crabmeat, onion, and cayenne pepper. Spoon into the casserole and sprinkle with the almonds. Bake, uncovered, for 10 to 15 minutes, until bubbly. Serve with crackers or melba toast.

NOTE: To soften cream cheese, remove from the foil wrapper and place on a microwave-safe dish. Microwave for 10 seconds at high power.

SWISS MUSHROOMS AU GRATIN

Offer these juicy baked mushrooms with slices of crusty French bread. Instead of white button mushrooms, you can use baby bellas, morels, oyster mushrooms, or other flavorful mushrooms.

SERVES 6

3 tablespoons butter, plus extra for the dish

2 tablespoons minced shallots or green onions (white and green parts)

1½ pounds mushrooms, sliced

1 teaspoon salt

1 teaspoon fresh lemon juice

2 tablespoons sherry

1½ cups heavy cream, divided

3 large eggs

Pinch of ground nutmeg

⅛ teaspoon pepper

¼ cup shredded Swiss cheese

1. Preheat the oven to 375°F. Butter a 1½-quart shallow casserole or gratin dish.

2. In a large skillet, melt the 3 tablespoons butter, add the shallots, and sauté for 2 minutes, stirring. Stir in the mushrooms, salt, lemon juice, and sherry. Cook for 10 minutes, or until the liquid has been absorbed. Add 1 cup cream. Bring to a boil and continue boiling for about 5 minutes, or until the cream is reduced to a thick sauce.

3. In a medium bowl, beat the eggs and the remaining ½ cup cream. Stir the mushroom mixture into the egg mixture and transfer to the buttered dish. Sprinkle with the nutmeg, pepper, and Swiss cheese.

4. Bake, uncovered, for 15 to 20 minutes, or until bubbly.

SHIITAKE MUSHROOMS WITH GRUYÈRE

These mushrooms are just a little slurpy and sloppy, but so delicious! They are actually easier to serve as a first course at a sit-down meal.

SERVES 6 TO 8

7 tablespoons butter

1 pound shiitake or baby bella mushrooms, sliced

¼ teaspoon ground nutmeg

Salt

Pepper

¼ cup heavy cream

6 to 8 slices French bread, about 1 inch thick

½ cup shredded Gruyère or Swiss cheese

Chopped fresh parsley for garnish

1. Preheat the oven to 400°F. In a large skillet, melt the butter over medium heat. Add the mushrooms and sauté for 10 minutes, or until the liquid has evaporated. Reduce the heat to medium-low and stir in the nutmeg, salt and pepper to taste, and cream. Cook until thickened.

2. Arrange the bread slices in a shallow 1½-quart casserole or an 8-inch square baking dish. Make a slight indentation in the center of each slice. Spoon the mushroom mixture over the slices and sprinkle with the cheese.

3. Bake, uncovered, for 10 minutes, or until the cheese is melted. Garnish with the parsley.

CRAB AND SWEET CURRY QUICHE

Curry powder is a blend of twenty or more spices and herbs, including cardamom, cloves, cinnamon, coriander, mace, and nutmeg. These are all "sweet" spices, as opposed to hot spices like chiles and black pepper. Select a mild curry powder for this recipe to bring out the flavor of the crab. Serve the quiche cut into small triangles for an appetizer or in larger wedges for a first course. It also makes a delicious main course for a light lunch or supper.

SERVES 8

1 recipe Flaky Pastry (page 32)

2 tablespoons minced shallots

1 tablespoon butter

1 teaspoon sweet curry powder

1 cup shredded cooked crabmeat, well drained

2 tablespoons minced fresh chives

1 tablespoon all-purpose flour

1½ cups shredded Swiss cheese, divided

3 large eggs

1 cup light cream or half-and-half

½ teaspoon salt

Dash of Tabasco sauce

1. Prepare the pastry and chill in the refrigerator. Preheat the oven to 350°F.

2. *While the pastry is chilling, prepare the filling:* Sauté the shallots in the butter for about 2 minutes and add the curry powder. Transfer to a medium bowl and add the crabmeat, chives, and flour.

3. Roll out the chilled pastry into a 12-inch circle and transfer to a 9-inch tart or pie pan. Trim and crimp the edges.

4. Spread half the cheese in the bottom of the pastry shell. Top with the crab mixture and sprinkle with the remaining cheese.

5. In a small bowl, whisk together the eggs, cream, salt, and Tabasco sauce, and pour over the filling in the pastry shell.

6. Bake for 35 to 40 minutes, or until the filling is lightly browned and a knife inserted near the center comes out clean. Serve warm or at room temperature.

BEEF AND ANCHO CHILE CHEESE DIP

An ancho chile is a broad dried chile, 3 to 4 inches long, which ranges in flavor from mild to hot. In its fresh, green state, the ancho is called a "poblano" chile. You can either pulverize the dried, deep-red pod (seeds removed) into a powder yourself, or you can buy it in powder form. One good source is Penzeys, a nationally known purveyor of spices. This appetizer will remind your guests of nachos, a favorite appetizer of kids and teens alike.

SERVES 8

1 pound lean ground beef

1 tablespoon ancho chile powder

Salt

½ teaspoon dried marjoram

1 can (15½ ounces) seasoned chili beans

1 can (10 ounces) diced tomatoes and green chiles with their juice

2 cups crumbled queso fresco (Mexican farmers' cheese) or feta cheese, divided

1. Preheat the oven to 350°F. Coat a 1½-quart shallow casserole with cooking spray.

2. In a large nonstick skillet, cook the beef over medium heat, stirring to separate the clumps of meat, until no pink remains, about 10 minutes.

3. In a large bowl, combine the cooked beef with the chile powder, salt to taste, the marjoram, chili beans, tomatoes and chiles with their juice, and 1 cup of the cheese. Spread out in the prepared casserole and sprinkle the remaining cup of cheese evenly over the top. (At this point you can cover and refrigerate the dip for up to 1 day. Add an extra 5 minutes to the baking time.)

4. Before serving, bake, uncovered, until the cheese is melted, 20 to 25 minutes. Serve hot with tortilla chips, crackers, bread, or freshly cut vegetables.

EGGPLANT AND GARLIC SLATHER

A slather is something you spread generously on crisp croutons or toasted slices of French bread. Try this as a sauce for pasta, as well. To allow the flavors to develop, make this slather ahead and refrigerate for an hour or two, or even a day in advance.

SERVES 8

1 large eggplant, or 5 to 7 small Japanese eggplants (1½ pounds total)

2 teaspoons olive oil, divided

2 whole heads garlic

2 tablespoons balsamic vinegar

¼ cup chopped fresh basil

2 to 3 tablespoons nonfat plain yogurt

½ teaspoon salt

¼ teaspoon pepper

⅔ cup grated Parmesan cheese, divided

French bread slices, toasted, for serving

1. Preheat the oven to 350°F. Coat a shallow 4-cup casserole with cooking spray.

2. Cut a few slits in the eggplant(s). Rub all over with 1 teaspoon olive oil and place in a shallow roasting pan or on a rimmed baking sheet. Drizzle the garlic heads with the remaining 1 teaspoon olive oil. Wrap them in foil and place on the same tray as the eggplants.

3. Bake the garlic and eggplant until the eggplant wrinkles and starts to collapse, about 1 hour. Remove from the oven. Cool enough to be able to handle.

4. Cut the eggplant in half and scrape the pulp into the bowl of a food processor. Squeeze the garlic cloves out of their skins and into the food processor. Add the vinegar, basil, yogurt, salt, and pepper. Process until almost smooth.

5. Spread half the puree in the casserole dish. Top with half the Parmesan cheese, and spread the remaining puree over the cheese. Sprinkle with the remaining Parmesan cheese. (The slather can be made up to this point 12 hours in advance. Cover and refrigerate until ready to bake.)

6. Before serving, preheat the oven to 400°F. Bake the slather, uncovered, for 10 to 15 minutes, until bubbly. Serve hot with slices of French bread.

ROASTED GARLIC AND ONION BEAN SPREAD

The length of this recipe makes it look difficult. It is actually simple, especially if you roast the garlic and onion the day before you make the dip. They infuse this delicious hot dip with subtle flavors.

SERVES 10

2 cans (16 ounces each) pinto beans, rinsed and drained

3 tablespoons olive oil

4 teaspoons chili powder

1 teaspoon ground cumin

1 large roasted yellow onion, chopped (see Note, facing page)

4 large cloves roasted garlic, chopped (see Note, facing page)

1 teaspoon Tabasco sauce

2 cups shredded Monterey Jack cheese, divided

Salt

Chopped fresh cilantro for garnish

Tortilla chips for serving

1. Preheat the oven to 400°F.

2. Puree the beans in a food processor.

3. Heat the olive oil in a heavy saucepan. Add the chili powder and cumin and stir over medium heat until aromatic. Add the pureed beans to the saucepan. Stir in the chopped roasted onion and garlic and cook, stirring, for 5 minutes.

4. Stir in the Tabasco and 1 cup of the cheese and season with salt to taste. Pour into a shallow 1½-quart casserole and sprinkle the remaining cup of cheese over the top. (The spread can be covered and refrigerated at this point for up to 6 to 8 hours.)

5. Before serving, place the casserole in the oven until heated through and the cheese is melted. Sprinkle with chopped cilantro and serve with tortilla chips.

○○○○○

NOTES: To roast the onion, rub a large yellow-skinned onion with oil (do not peel the onion). Wrap in heavy-duty aluminum foil, crimping it at the top to close tightly. Place in a preheated 400°F oven for 1 to 1½ hours, or until the onion is soft. Allow to cool in the foil before peeling and chopping.

To roast the garlic, cut the top off of a large, firm head of garlic, exposing the tips of the garlic cloves. Place on a square of heavy-duty aluminum foil. Drizzle with some olive oil and sprinkle with a little salt. Wrap the garlic in the foil, and tightly crimp the top to close. Place in a preheated 400°F oven for 30 to 40 minutes, or until soft. Cool, then press gently on the bottom to push the soft roasted cloves from their skins.

DILLED CHIPPED BEEF DIP

Chipped beef, the wafer-thin slices of salted and smoked dried beef, is also referred to as "dried beef," and usually comes packed in small jars. Here, rather than mixing it with the usual cream sauce, we've made it into an appetizer, which is tasty on crackers or lavash.

SERVES 10

2 tablespoons butter

1 small onion, chopped

1 tablespoon fresh lemon juice

¾ cup sour cream

1 package (8 ounces) cream cheese, softened (see Note)

1 teaspoon dried dill weed

1 jar (3 ounces) dried beef, chopped

½ cup chopped pecans

1. Preheat the oven to 350°F.

2. In a large skillet, melt the butter and sauté the onion over medium-low heat until tender, about 5 minutes. Add the lemon juice and cook for 2 minutes.

3. Add the sour cream, cream cheese, dill weed, and dried beef to the skillet and stir until all of the ingredients are well combined. Pour the mixture into an 8-inch square baking dish and top with the pecans.

4. Bake, uncovered, for 15 to 20 minutes until bubbly.

○○○○○

NOTE: To soften cream cheese, remove from the foil wrapper and place on a microwave-safe dish. Microwave for 10 seconds at high power.

QUICK AND EASY CHILE CON QUESO DIP

You can assemble the ingredients for this party dip, cover it, and refrigerate until an hour or so before your party. Slip it into the oven, and it will be ready when your first guests arrive.

SERVES 10

- 2 cups shredded Monterey Jack cheese
- 1 package (8 ounces) cream cheese, softened (see Note, facing page)
- 1 can (10 ounces) diced tomatoes and green chiles
- ½ cup picante sauce or salsa (mild, medium, or hot)
- Tortilla chips for serving

1. Preheat the oven to 350°F.

2. Combine all of the ingredients except the tortilla chips in a 1-quart casserole. Cover and bake for 20 to 25 minutes, until the cheese is melted and the dip is bubbly.

3. Serve with crisp tortilla chips.

JALAPEÑO CHILE CON QUESO

Jalapeño pepper can make this version of chile con queso spicy hot. Remember, though, when handling hot peppers, to wear rubber gloves and keep your hands away from your face, especially your eyes!

SERVES 10

2 tablespoons butter

2 green onions, minced (white and green parts)

1 poblano pepper, seeded and diced

1 teaspoon ground cumin

1 large tomato, diced

1 can (4 ounces) diced green chiles

1 jalapeño pepper, seeded and diced (optional)

1 package (8 ounces) cream cheese, cubed

½ cup heavy cream or sour cream

1 cup shredded Monterey Jack cheese

Chopped fresh cilantro for garnish

Tortilla chips or raw vegetables for serving

1. Preheat the oven to 350°F.

2. Melt the butter in a small skillet and add the green onions and poblano pepper. Sauté for about 5 minutes, until tender.

3. In a 1-quart casserole, combine the green onion mixture, cumin, tomato, diced chiles, jalapeño pepper (if using), cream cheese, and heavy or sour cream. (At this point the casserole can be covered and refrigerated for up to 1 day. Add 5 minutes to the baking time.)

4. Bake, uncovered, for 30 minutes, or until bubbly. Sprinkle with the Monterey Jack cheese and cilantro. Serve hot with tortilla chips or raw vegetables for dipping.

BEAN AND BURGER SPREAD

Think of this spread when you are planning a large party or picnic, or if you need to bring something to a potluck affair. This is an appetizer that appeals to meat-loving teens. To reduce the saltiness, substitute low-sodium cheese for the Cheddar and diced canned tomatoes for the taco sauce.

SERVES 12 TO 16

- 1 can (16 ounces) refried beans
- 1 pound lean ground beef
- 1 medium sweet onion, diced, divided
- 1 can (4 ounces) diced green chiles
- ½ cup sliced black olives, plus more for garnish
- 2½ cups shredded Cheddar or Jack cheese
- 1 cup taco or chile sauce (mild, medium, or hot)
- Tortilla chips for serving

1. Preheat the oven to 350°F.

2. Spread the bottom of a 9-by-13-inch baking dish with the refried beans.

3. In a large nonstick skillet, brown the beef and half of the onion over medium-high heat.

4. Spread the beef and onion mixture over the refried beans. Sprinkle with the green chiles, ½ cup olives, the cheese, and the remaining half of the onion. Drizzle with taco sauce. (The casserole can be covered and refrigerated at this point for up to 12 hours. Add 5 to 10 minutes to the baking time.)

5. Bake, uncovered, for 20 to 30 minutes, until bubbly. Garnish with more black olives and serve with tortilla chips.

BROCCOLI AND PARMESAN SLATHER

This hot, savory spread is perfect to serve buffet-style with rounds of toast, crackers, or raw vegetables.

SERVES 12

1 package (10 ounces) frozen chopped broccoli, or 1 medium head fresh broccoli

1 cup light or regular mayonnaise

1 tablespoon fresh lemon juice

1 tablespoon dried basil leaves

1 teaspoon chili powder

½ cup chopped fresh chives

½ cup chopped fresh parsley

1 cup grated Parmesan cheese

1. Preheat the oven to 350°F.

2. If using frozen broccoli, cook according to package directions and drain. If using fresh broccoli, cut off and discard tough ends from stalks. Peel the remaining stems if the skin is tough. Cook in boiling water for 10 minutes, or until tender; drain and chop.

3. In a food processor with the steel blade in place, combine the broccoli, mayonnaise, lemon juice, basil, chili powder, chives, parsley, and Parmesan cheese. Transfer to a shallow 1-quart casserole.

4. Bake, uncovered, for 20 minutes, or until heated through and browned on top. Serve hot.

Variation: Try this with cauliflower, and substitute shredded Cheddar for the Parmesan.

CHILE-CHEESE OMELET SQUARES

These are satisfying little bites of omelet spiked with chiles and hot pepper cheese. You can make these squares ahead of time, wrap them well, and refrigerate. Reheat just until warm before serving.

SERVES 12

- 8 large eggs, beaten
- ½ pound mushrooms, sliced
- 1 can (4 ounces) chopped green chiles
- 4 slices bacon, cooked and diced, or ½ cup diced cooked ham
- 1 cup shredded spicy pepper cheese

1. Preheat the oven to 350°F. Coat a shallow 1-quart casserole with cooking spray.

2. In a large bowl, whisk together the eggs, mushrooms, chiles, bacon, and cheese and pour the mixture into the casserole dish. Bake, uncovered, for 20 minutes, or until set. Cool and cut into 1-inch squares. Serve with toothpicks.

CURRIED MUSHROOMS

Here is a slightly different take on a curry. You can serve these mushrooms as a vegetarian main dish as well as a first course.

SERVES 12

4 tablespoons butter

2 cups chopped onions

2 cloves garlic, minced

1 cup chopped celery

1½ pounds mushrooms

1½ teaspoons salt

1 teaspoon ground cumin

1 teaspoon ground cinnamon

1 teaspoon ground turmeric

1 teaspoon grated fresh ginger

½ teaspoon dry mustard

½ teaspoon ground cloves

2 large cooking apples, such as Fuji, Gala, or Granny Smith, peeled and chopped

3 large tomatoes, peeled, seeded, and chopped

3 tablespoons shredded coconut

1 tablespoon honey

2 tablespoons fresh lemon juice

Crisp toast rounds or toasted pita triangles for serving

Sliced or slivered almonds, toasted, for garnish (see Note)

1. Preheat the oven to 350°F.

2. In a large skillet, melt the butter and add the onions and garlic. Sauté for 5 minutes, or until tender. Transfer to a 2-quart casserole and add the celery. Remove the stems from the mushrooms and chop the stems. Stir the stems, mushroom caps, and salt into the casserole.

3. Bake, covered, for 30 minutes or until the mushrooms have released their juices.

4. Meanwhile, in a small bowl, mix together the cumin, cinnamon, turmeric, ginger, mustard, and cloves. Stir into the mushroom mixture and add the apples, tomatoes, coconut, honey, and lemon juice. Return the casserole to the oven and bake, uncovered, for 25 minutes, or until all the ingredients are just tender; do not overcook. Cover and let stand 10 minutes before serving. Spoon onto crisp toast rounds or pita triangles and garnish with toasted almonds.

○○○○○

NOTE: To toast the almonds, spread them out on a cookie sheet and toast in a 350°F oven for about 10 minutes, stirring occasionally, until the nuts are fragrant and lightly browned.

JARLSBERG CHEESE SPREAD

The nutty flavor of Jarlsberg cheese, melted into a baked spread, goes equally well with bread, crackers, or sliced fresh apple. The last time I made this, I thought I had Jarlsberg in the fridge, but it was actually a Swedish fontina. I used it anyway, with excellent results.

SERVES 12

2 cups shredded or diced Jarlsberg cheese

2 tablespoons minced red onion

½ cup mayonnaise

1. Preheat the oven to 400°F. Coat a shallow 1-quart casserole with cooking spray.

2. In a medium bowl, mix the cheese, onion, and mayonnaise and spread in the bottom of the casserole. Bake, uncovered, for 15 minutes, or until hot and bubbly.

BAKED MUSHROOMS WITH GARLIC AND CHEESE

Provide a small container of toothpicks and some crusty French bread for serving these delicious, cheesy mushroom tidbits. If the mushrooms are large, cut the slices into quarters; if they're medium-size, just halve them. Tiny button mushrooms can be left whole.

SERVES 12

1 pound mushrooms, sliced

4 large cloves garlic, sliced

7 tablespoons butter, plus more for the dish

1 teaspoon kosher salt

½ teaspoon pepper

½ cup grated Parmesan cheese

Slices of French bread for serving

1. Preheat the oven to 400°F. Butter a shallow 1½-quart casserole.

2. Arrange the mushrooms in the casserole in an even layer and top with the sliced garlic. Dot with the butter and sprinkle with salt and pepper. Bake, uncovered, for 20 minutes, or until bubbly. Sprinkle with the cheese.

3. Serve the mushrooms with slices of French bread.

PARMESAN AND SUN-DRIED TOMATO QUICHE

For a tasty filling that is relatively low in fat, use evaporated milk. Don't use skim, though—a little fat carries flavor!

SERVES 12

FOR THE PASTRY:

1 cup all-purpose flour

½ teaspoon salt

¼ cup vegetable or canola oil

2 to 3 tablespoons milk

FOR THE FILLING:

2 tablespoons unsalted butter

½ cup chopped onions

½ cup sun-dried tomatoes, chopped (not oil-packed)

½ cup grated Parmesan cheese

4 large eggs

2 cups light cream or evaporated milk

½ teaspoon salt (optional)

⅛ teaspoon ground nutmeg

1. Preheat the oven to 425°F.

2. *To make the pastry:* With a fork, stir together the flour, salt, and oil in a medium bowl until the mixture is crumbly. Stir in enough milk to moisten the flour and form moist crumbs. Flatten into a disk and place between sheets of waxed paper. Chill for 10 to 15 minutes. Roll out the pastry into a 9- or 10-inch square to fit an 8- or 9-inch square baking pan, preferably with removable sides. Transfer to the pan and crimp the edges. With a fork, pierce several holes in the crust and bake for 10 minutes. Remove from the oven. If the dough has puffed up, gently press down.

3. *To make the filling:* Melt the butter in a heavy nonstick skillet over medium heat. Add the onions and sauté for 5 minutes, or until softened.

4. Spread the onions in the bottom of the partially baked crust. Sprinkle with the sun-dried tomatoes and Parmesan cheese.

5. Whisk the eggs, cream, salt (if using), and nutmeg in a medium bowl and pour over the onion mixture. Bake the quiche for 15 minutes at 425°F. Lower the temperature to 350°F and bake for another 25 to 30 minutes, or until set and the tip of a knife comes out clean when inserted in the center.

BAKED RICOTTA WITH GARLIC AND HERBS

In this easy and delicious casserole, the ricotta bakes down into a creamy cheese sauce. It makes a perfect appetizer for a buffet-style meal.

SERVES 12

1 tablespoon olive oil

2 cups ricotta cheese

1 teaspoon salt

½ teaspoon pepper

4 cloves garlic, minced

¼ cup chopped fresh herbs, such as basil, rosemary, and thyme

¼ cup heavy cream

12 slices French bread, toasted or grilled, for serving

1. Preheat the oven to 300°F.

2. Coat a 1-quart casserole with the olive oil.

3. In a large bowl, stir the ricotta together with the salt, pepper, garlic, herbs, and cream. Transfer to the casserole. Bake, uncovered, for about 15 minutes, until the cheese is creamy and hot. Serve with the French bread slices.

SPINACH AND PARMESAN SLATHER

Put these ingredients together in a pretty little casserole dish so that it will be ready to pop into the oven 15 minutes before your guests arrive.

SERVES ABOUT 12

- 1 bag (9 ounces) fresh spinach leaves
- 1 cup grated Parmesan cheese
- ½ cup regular or low-fat mayonnaise
- ½ cup regular or low-fat sour cream
- 1 clove garlic, minced
- 1 tablespoon fresh lemon juice
- 1 tablespoon Dijon mustard
- 1 teaspoon dried basil
- ½ teaspoon salt
- ⅛ teaspoon cayenne pepper
- ½ cup pine nuts
- Slices of crusty French bread or freshly cut vegetables for serving

1. Preheat the oven to 400°F. Butter a shallow 1- to 1½-quart casserole.

2. Put the spinach in a large bowl and cover with boiling water. Press the leaves down into the water until they wilt. Drain the spinach well and squeeze out all the liquid.

3. Combine the spinach, Parmesan, mayonnaise, sour cream, garlic, lemon juice, mustard, basil, salt, and cayenne in a food processor fitted with the steel blade. Process until the spinach is finely chopped, but not pureed. Alternatively, chop the spinach by hand and combine with the remaining ingredients except the pine nuts and bread slices. Spoon into the buttered casserole and sprinkle with the pine nuts. (At this point the casserole can be covered and refrigerated overnight. Add 5 minutes to the baking time.)

4. Bake, uncovered, for 15 minutes, or until lightly browned. Serve hot with the bread or vegetables.

HERBED CHICKEN TERRINE WITH EXOTIC FRUIT SALSA

Each slice of this beautiful meat loaf reveals a round of white chicken breast, surrounded by a puree of spinach and herbs. It is absolutely perfect for a summertime dinner party and ideal because you can make this terrine up to 3 days ahead of time. It needs to be chilled so that it can be cut into slices for serving. To save time, you can skip steps 1 and 2 and buy a rotisserie chicken breast from the supermarket. The recipe is a little fussy, but really worth the effort!

SERVES 12

1 whole chicken (3½ to 4 pounds)

1 lime, halved

1 medium onion

2 tablespoons butter, cut into pieces

3 cups baby spinach leaves, divided

Leaves of 8 sprigs fresh tarragon

⅔ cup heavy cream

3 large eggs

1½ to 2 teaspoons salt

1 teaspoon freshly ground black pepper

1 pound sliced bacon

FOR THE EXOTIC FRUIT SALSA:

½ cup fresh orange juice

1 cup finely diced mango

1 cup finely diced papaya

1 cup finely diced pineapple

1 Scotch bonnet chile, stem and seeds discarded, minced

½ cup finely diced red onion

3 tablespoons olive oil

Salt

Pepper

1. To roast the chicken, preheat the oven to 400°F. Or preheat a charcoal grill and bank the coals for indirect heat.

2. Wash the chicken and pat dry with paper towels. Squeeze lime juice over the chicken and in the cavity. Put the lime halves into the cavity along with the onion. Dot the chicken with butter. Place the chicken on a rack in a roasting pan and roast in the oven for 1½ hours, or until a leg jiggles easily and an instant-read thermometer inserted in the thigh reads 185°F. Or grill for 1½ hours, covered. Melt the butter and brush the chicken 2 or 3 times while grilling. Remove from the oven or grill and cool. Reduce the oven temperature to 325°F (or preheat the oven if you were grilling the chicken).

3. Remove the breast meat in 2 big chunks and set aside. Remove the skin and bones from the chicken carcass and put the meat into a food processor fitted with the steel blade.

Add the roasted onion, 1 cup of the spinach leaves, the tarragon leaves, cream, eggs, salt, and pepper. Puree until smooth.

4. If you have one, line a narrow, loaf-shaped terrine with a tight-fitting lid with bacon slices. Otherwise, line a regular loaf pan. Spread 1 cup of the remaining baby spinach leaves evenly over the bottom of the terrine, covering the bacon.

5. Spread half of the pureed mixture over the spinach layer and top with the breast meat (tear into smaller pieces if necessary), so that there is a continual strip of the breast meat from one end of the terrine to the other. Top with the remaining pureed mixture. Spread the remaining 1 cup spinach leaves over the top.

6. Lap the ends of the bacon pieces over the top (they will not entirely cover it). Cover the top of the terrine with a strip of parchment or waxed paper. Place the cover on top to seal the terrine, or cover tightly with foil.

7. Set into a large roasting pan and add enough hot water to come halfway up the sides of the terrine or loaf pan. Bake for 2 hours.

8. *Meanwhile, make the Exotic Fruit Salsa:* In a small saucepan, bring the orange juice to a boil over medium-high heat and cook, stirring, until reduced to about 2 tablespoons. Remove from the heat and allow to cool slightly. Combine the mango, papaya, pineapple, chile, onion, and olive oil in a large bowl and stir in the juice. Season with salt and pepper.

9. Cool the terrine completely, unmold, and cut into thin slices. Serve with spoonfuls of the salsa.

TERRINE OF HERBS AND PORK

Many years ago, I attended a weeklong series of cooking classes with Simone Beck (coauthor, with Julia Child, of the famed *Mastering the Art of French Cooking,* volumes I and II). I think this is the only recipe that has remained in my repertoire, and even these many years later it is still a favorite summertime "meat loaf." I've adjusted and changed the recipe over the years. I like to bake this in a narrow enameled cast-iron terrine with a lid. After it has cooked and cooled, you can cut as many slices as you like and refrigerate the remainder. Because of all the herbs and spices, it keeps well and is wonderful for an impromptu lunch, served with a salad.

SERVES 16

1 pound reduced-sodium sliced bacon, divided

1 pound lean ground pork

1 cup minced onion

2 cloves garlic, minced

1 package (10 ounces) frozen chopped spinach, cooked and drained

1 tablespoon chopped fresh tarragon leaves, or 2 teaspoons dried

1 teaspoon fresh rosemary leaves, or ½ teaspoon dried

1 teaspoon fresh oregano leaves, or ½ teaspoon dried

1 teaspoon fresh thyme leaves, or ½ teaspoon dried

1 teaspoon fresh or dried marjoram leaves

2 teaspoons salt

½ teaspoon pepper

¼ teaspoon ground nutmeg

½ cup dry sherry

2 tablespoons unflavored gelatin

1 cup heavy cream

4 large eggs, lightly beaten

½ pound boiled ham, cut into ½-inch dice

1. Preheat the oven to 350°F. Line a 1½-quart loaf pan or terrine with the bacon slices, overlapping them slightly. You'll have about 4 slices left over. Cut them into ½-inch pieces and cook in a skillet over medium heat until crisp. Remove the bacon from the skillet and reserve; pour out all but 2 tablespoons of the bacon fat.

2. Put the pork into a large bowl. Add the onion and garlic to the bacon fat and sauté over medium heat for 3 minutes,

stirring. Add to the pork along with the spinach, all of the herbs, the salt, pepper, nutmeg, sherry, and gelatin. (The gelatin does not need to be softened first.) Mix well and add the cream and eggs.

3. Turn half of the mixture into the loaf pan and pat down evenly. Top with the cooked bacon and boiled ham and press down slightly into the meat mixture. Spread the remaining meat mixture on top and lap the ends of the bacon over the top of the meat.

4. Cover with a strip of parchment or waxed paper. If your pan has no lid, cover tightly with foil. Otherwise, place the lid on top of the parchment paper.

5. Place the loaf pan or terrine inside a large roasting pan and add 1 inch of boiling water to the larger pan. Bake the terrine for 1 hour and 45 minutes, or until an instant-read thermometer inserted near the center registers 165 to 170°F. Remove from the oven and cool on a rack. Place a weight on top of the terrine, ideally something rectangular that will press the loaf evenly. I often place a narrow cutting board on top and then weight it down with a couple of cans of vegetables. Chill for at least 4 hours, or overnight.

6. To serve, turn the terrine out onto a serving plate or cutting board and slice. Refrigerate any leftover terrine for up to 4 days or freeze for up to 1 month.

SWEET ONION, ROSEMARY, AND CHEESE SLATHER

Hot spreads such as this one are so appealing and yet easy to put together. The sweet onions are juicy and mild, so even though they are plentiful, they don't overpower the spread.

SERVES 16

2 tablespoons butter

2 large sweet onions (about 2½ pounds total), coarsely chopped

1 clove garlic, minced

2 cups shredded Swiss cheese

1 cup mayonnaise

1 teaspoon dried rosemary, crushed

½ teaspoon Tabasco sauce

½ cup shredded Parmesan cheese

Crackers for serving

1. Preheat the oven to 350°F. Coat a shallow 1½-quart casserole with cooking spray.

2. In a large nonstick skillet over medium-high heat, melt the butter and sauté the onions and garlic until tender, 20 to 25 minutes. Remove from the heat. Add the Swiss cheese, mayonnaise, rosemary, and Tabasco sauce.

3. Transfer to the casserole dish. Bake, uncovered, for 20 minutes until lightly browned. Sprinkle with the Parmesan cheese and serve with crackers.

SUN-DRIED TOMATO AND ARTICHOKE SLATHER

Slather toasted slices of French bread with this creamy, hot spread. It makes a lot, so when I prepare it, I freeze half and am happy to have an appetizer in reserve for another party. Thaw the frozen portion for an hour or two at room temperature before baking.

SERVES ABOUT 24

1 can (14 ounces) artichoke hearts, drained

½ cup julienned oil-packed sun-dried tomatoes, drained

1 cup grated Parmesan cheese

1 cup low-fat sour cream

1 clove garlic, minced

1 tablespoon fresh lemon juice

1 teaspoon Dijon mustard

2 cups shredded Jarlsberg, Gruyère, or Swiss cheese

⅛ teaspoon cayenne pepper

¼ cup pine nuts

French bread slices, toasted, or freshly cut vegetables for serving

1. Preheat the oven to 400°F. Butter a 4-cup shallow casserole.

2. Combine the artichokes, sun-dried tomatoes, Parmesan cheese, sour cream, garlic, lemon juice, and mustard in a food processor fitted with the steel blade. Process until all ingredients are coarsely chopped. Mix in the cheese and cayenne.

3. Turn the mixture into the casserole and spread out evenly. Sprinkle with the pine nuts and bake, uncovered, for 15 minutes, or until lightly browned. Serve hot with the bread or vegetables.

Chapter 3
NO-KNEAD CASSEROLE BREADS

The casserole breads in this chapter are for cooks who are not only short of time, but also have had inhibitions about bread baking. The upside of baking your own breads is that you know exactly what is in them. You can avoid fat, especially trans fats, which have proven to be unhealthy.

These are old-fashioned breads that require no kneading. Some, like the spoon breads, are pudding-like. Most, however, can be sliced. What separates them from most yeast breads is that they have a high ratio of liquid to flour and therefore are beaten, rather than kneaded.

Because a casserole bread is almost a batter, the bread often has a rather rough surface, and may have a moist, open texture when sliced. All are irresistible, smell wonderful when they're baking, and are healthy breads to serve your family and guests.

CORNMEAL SPOON BREAD

Spoon breads are traditionally served as a side dish. They are scooped out of the casserole dish with a spoon, but are often eaten with a fork. Spoon bread goes especially well with roasted chicken, or it can be served with a cheese sauce as a luncheon main course. If you serve it with fruit salad on the side, you will have an old-fashioned "ladies' luncheon menu."

SERVES 4 TO 6

2 tablespoons butter, plus extra for the dish

2 cups milk

1 teaspoon sugar

1 teaspoon salt

⅔ cup yellow cornmeal

4 large eggs, separated

1. Preheat the oven to 375°F. Butter a 2-quart casserole.

2. Combine the milk, the 2 tablespoons butter, the sugar, and salt in a saucepan. Bring to a boil and slowly add the cornmeal, stirring constantly. Cook for 3 to 5 minutes, or until thickened. Remove from the heat and let cool slightly.

3. With a fork, beat the egg yolks in a small bowl. Add a small portion of the hot mixture to the eggs, and stir well. Return the egg yolk mixture to the pan and mix well.

4. Beat the egg whites in a medium bowl until soft peaks form, then fold into the cornmeal mixture. Transfer to the buttered casserole and bake for 35 minutes, or until firm.

IRISH WHEAT AND OATMEAL BREAD

Consider serving this grainy bread with a hot bowl of vegetable soup. The Irish often leaven whole-grain breads like this one with baking powder or baking soda. This is a slightly heavy bread, which is delicious cut into thin slices and slathered with butter.

SERVES 10

1 tablespoon butter, melted, plus extra for the pan

2 cups all-purpose flour, plus extra for dusting

1 cup whole-wheat flour

1 ¼ cups quick-cooking or old-fashioned rolled oats

1½ tablespoons baking powder

1 tablespoon salt

1 large egg

¼ cup honey

1½ cups milk

1. Preheat the oven to 350°F. Butter a 5-by-9-inch bread pan and dust with the all-purpose flour.

2. In a large bowl, mix the 2 cups all-purpose flour, the whole-wheat flour, rolled oats, baking powder, and salt. In a medium bowl, mix the egg, honey, and milk.

3. Pour the liquid ingredients into the dry ingredients and stir together until the dry ingredients are moistened. The mixture will not be smooth.

4. Transfer to the prepared bread pan and bake for 1 hour and 15 minutes, or until crusty and a skewer inserted near the center comes out clean. Drizzle the 1 tablespoon melted butter over the hot loaf and turn out onto a wire rack to cool.

POLENTA SPOON BREAD

More like a soufflé than a bread, polenta spoon bread is delicious with a simple meal of roast chicken and steamed vegetables. Serve it with melted butter, gravy, or a white sauce flavored with lemon juice (see page 18).

SERVES 6

- 1 tablespoon butter, plus extra for the dish
- 1½ cups water
- 1½ cups polenta or cornmeal
- 1 teaspoon salt
- 1½ cups milk, divided
- 2 large eggs, separated
- 2 teaspoons baking powder
- Extra butter, white sauce, or gravy for serving

1. Preheat the oven to 400°F. Butter a 1½-quart casserole or soufflé dish.

2. Bring the water to a boil in a medium saucepan. Combine the polenta and salt and stir into the boiling water. Cook, stirring, until thickened, about 15 minutes. Add 1 cup of the milk and cook, stirring, until smooth, about 5 minutes.

3. Beat the remaining ½ cup milk and the egg yolks together. Add a small amount of the polenta mixture to temper the egg yolks, and stir well. Stir into the hot polenta mixture in the saucepan. Mix in the 1 tablespoon butter and the baking powder and stir until smooth.

4. Beat the egg whites with an electric mixer in a medium bowl until stiff and fold into the mixture. Pour the batter into the prepared dish and bake until puffed and golden, 35 to 40 minutes. Serve hot with butter, white sauce, or gravy.

CINNAMON BUBBLE BREAD

The "bubbles" in this loaf of bread are little rounds of dough, which are rolled in cinnamon and sugar, and then piled into a baking pan. The bread tastes a lot like cinnamon rolls, and is fun to serve for breakfast or brunch, or with coffee. Use two forks or a pair of tongs to pull apart the bubbles.

SERVES 8 TO 10

6 tablespoons butter, melted, divided, plus extra for the dish

1 cup warm water (105 to 115°F)

2 packages (¼ ounce each) active dry yeast

2 tablespoons plus 1 cup sugar, divided

1 cup milk, scalded and cooled to lukewarm

2 teaspoons salt

4½ cups all-purpose flour, divided

2 tablespoons ground cinnamon

1. Generously butter a deep 2-quart casserole. Pour the warm water into a large bowl and stir in the yeast and the 2 tablespoons sugar. Let stand until foamy, about 5 minutes.

2. Add the milk, salt, 4 tablespoons of the melted butter, 1 cup of the flour, and ½ cup sugar; beat until smooth. Gradually beat in the remaining flour to make a stiff, satiny, smooth dough.

3. Cover with a kitchen towel and let rise until doubled in size, about 45 minutes. Turn out the dough onto a lightly oiled work surface. Divide the dough into quarters. Divide each quarter into quarters again, to make 16 pieces. Cut each of the pieces in half to make 32 pieces total.

4. Pour the remaining 2 tablespoons melted butter into a small dish. In another small dish mix the remaining ½ cup of sugar and the cinnamon. Roll each piece of dough first in the butter and then in the cinnamon sugar. Place the dough pieces in the buttered casserole in even layers. Cover with a kitchen towel and let rise in a warm place until doubled in size, about 45 minutes.

5. Meanwhile, preheat the oven to 375°F. Bake the bread for 35 to 45 minutes, or until browned and a skewer inserted in the center of the loaf comes out clean. Cool in the casserole for 5 minutes. Invert onto a serving dish and serve warm, pulling apart the pieces.

WHOLE-WHEAT BUBBLE BREAD

Here's another version of a healthy bubble bread, which is fabulous served hot from the oven. In the unlikely event that you have bread left over, you can freeze it in plastic bags. Or cut it into cubes and use it in a breakfast strata.

SERVES 8 TO 10

2 tablespoons butter at room temperature, plus extra for the dish

1 ¼ cups warm water (105 to 115°F)

1 package (¼ ounce) active dry yeast

2 tablespoons light or dark brown sugar

1½ teaspoons salt

2 large eggs

1½ cups whole-wheat flour

2 to 2½ cups all-purpose flour

½ cup (1 stick) butter, melted

1 cup wheat germ

1. Generously butter a 2-quart casserole or a 10-inch tube pan.

2. Pour the warm water into a large bowl; stir in the yeast and brown sugar. Let stand until foamy, about 5 minutes. Stir in the salt, 2 tablespoons of the softened butter, the eggs, and whole-wheat flour, and beat well. Let rest for 15 minutes, or until the mixture begins to look puffy.

3. Add 2 cups of the all-purpose flour gradually, beating to keep the mixture smooth, and adding enough flour to make a stiff dough. Let rest for another 15 minutes.

4. Turn out the dough onto a lightly floured surface. Clean and butter the bowl. Knead the dough for 10 minutes, or until smooth and satiny, adding all-purpose flour as necessary to keep the dough from sticking.

Put the dough into the buttered bowl, turning to coat the dough lightly with butter.

5. Cover with a kitchen towel, and let rise in a warm place until doubled in size, about 1 hour. Turn out onto a lightly oiled work surface. Divide the dough into quarters. Divide each quarter into quarters again, to make 16 pieces. Cut each of the pieces in half to make 32 pieces total.

6. Pour the melted butter into a small bowl. Pour the wheat germ into another small bowl. Shape each piece of dough into a round ball and roll in the melted butter and then in the wheat germ. Place the dough pieces in the buttered casserole in even layers. Cover and let rise in a warm place until doubled in size, 45 minutes to 1 hour.

7. Meanwhile, preheat the oven to 375°F. Bake the bread for 35 to 45 minutes, or until a skewer inserted in the center of the loaf comes out clean. Cool in the casserole for 5 minutes, then invert onto a serving dish. To serve, pull apart with forks.

HONEY MUSTARD BUBBLE BREAD

This bread is perfect with a soup or salad. There are many variations on bubble bread, which is also known as "monkey bread." Here, little balls of yeast dough are rolled in honey and mustard and piled into a baking pan to rise and bake.

SERVES 8 TO 10

4 tablespoons butter, melted, plus extra for the dish

1 cup warm water (105 to 115°F)

2 packages (¼ ounce each) active dry yeast

2 tablespoons sugar

1 cup milk, scalded and cooled to lukewarm

2 teaspoons salt

2 tablespoons olive oil

4½ cups all-purpose flour, divided

¼ cup honey

¼ cup Dijon mustard

1. Generously butter a deep 2-quart casserole. Pour the warm water into a large bowl and stir in the yeast and sugar. Let stand until foamy, about 5 minutes.

2. Add the milk, salt, olive oil, and 1 cup of the flour; beat until smooth. Gradually beat in the remaining flour to make a stiff, satiny, smooth dough.

3. Cover with a kitchen towel and let rise until doubled in size, about 45 minutes. Turn out the dough onto a lightly oiled work surface. Divide the dough into quarters. Divide each quarter into quarters again, to make 16 pieces. Cut each of the pieces in half to make 32 pieces total.

4. Mix the honey and mustard in a small dish. Roll each piece of dough in the honey and mustard mixture. Place the dough pieces in the buttered casserole in even layers. Drizzle with the 4 tablespoons of melted butter. Cover with a kitchen towel and let rise in a warm place until doubled in size, about 45 minutes.

5. Meanwhile, preheat the oven to 375°F. Bake the bread for 35 to 45 minutes, or until browned and a skewer inserted in the center of the loaf comes out clean. Cool in the casserole for 5 minutes. Invert onto a serving dish and serve warm, pulling apart the pieces.

CARAWAY AND CHEDDAR CASSEROLE BREAD

The caraway gives a distinctive flavor and texture to this cheesy batter bread, which is a no-knead, yeast-raised bread. Baked in a straight-sided 3-quart soufflé dish, it is very attractive.

SERVES 10

- 1½ cups warm water (105 to 115°F)
- 2 packages (¼ ounce each) active dry yeast
- 3 tablespoons dark brown sugar
- 1½ teaspoons salt
- 2 large eggs, at room temperature
- 1 cup rolled oats, quick-cooking or old-fashioned
- 3½ cups all-purpose flour, divided
- 2 cups shredded Cheddar cheese
- 3 tablespoons caraway seeds
- Melted butter for brushing the loaf

1. In a large bowl, dissolve the yeast in the warm water. Stir in the sugar, salt, eggs, and oats.

2. Add 1¾ cups of the flour and beat with an electric mixer for 2 to 3 minutes until the dough is very smooth. Cover with a kitchen towel and let rest for 5 minutes.

3. Add the cheese, caraway seeds, and 1 more cup flour and beat until well blended. Work in the remaining ¾ cup flour until it is no longer visible in the dough.

4. Cover and let rise in a warm place until doubled, about 30 minutes.

5. Stir down the dough and turn out into a greased 3-quart deep casserole or soufflé dish or two 8½-by-4½-inch loaf pans. Cover and let rise for 45 minutes to 1 hour, or until the batter reaches the top of the pan.

6. Meanwhile, preheat the oven to 350°F. Bake the bread for 45 minutes to 1 hour for the large round bread, or 35 to 40 minutes for the 2 loaves. Remove from the dish or pans and cool on a rack. Brush with melted butter.

CHEESE, OLIVE, AND PINE NUT CASSEROLE BREAD

Loaded with lots of flavors and textures, this no-knead bread can enhance almost any meal. It's perfect with a Mediterranean-style dinner. For the main course, choose a lasagna, pasta, or a Moroccan beef tagine.

SERVES 8 TO 10

½ cup warm water (105 to 115°F)

2 packages (¼ ounce each) active dry yeast

1 tablespoon sugar

1 teaspoon salt

2 tablespoons butter

1½ cups milk, scalded and cooled to lukewarm

1 large egg, beaten

4 cups all-purpose flour

¼ pound sharp Cheddar cheese, cut into ½-inch cubes (about 1 cup)

20 pitted mixed green and black olives (preferably kalamata for the black), halved

½ cup pine nuts

1. In a large bowl, combine the warm water, dry yeast, sugar, salt, butter, milk, and egg. Let stand for 5 minutes, or until the mixture begins to bubble.

2. Stir in the flour a little at a time until a very stiff batter forms. Beat with an electric mixer for 2 minutes. Cover with a kitchen towel and let stand for 15 minutes.

3. Stir in the Cheddar cheese, olives, and pine nuts. Butter a 3-quart round casserole or two 9-by-5-inch loaf pans. Turn the batter into the casserole or pans. Let rise for 45 minutes, or until the batter reaches the top of the dish or pans.

4. Meanwhile, preheat the oven to 375°F. Slash the top of the bread diagonally a few times with a sharp knife. Bake the 9-by-5-inch loaves for 35 to 40 minutes or the large loaf for 55 to 60 minutes, or until a wooden skewer inserted in the center of the loaf comes out clean and dry. Remove from the dish or pans and cool on a rack.

CINNAMON SALLY LUNN

Dating back to eighteenth-century England, a classic Sally Lunn is a slightly sweet, cakelike bread that is great for breakfast or brunch. Originally it was baked as a large bun, split horizontally, and slathered with thick clotted cream.

SERVES 8 TO 10

1 cup warm water (105 to 115°F)

2 packages (¼ ounce each) active dry yeast

¼ cup sugar

1 cup milk, scalded and cooled to room temperature

5 cups all-purpose flour, divided

2 large eggs, lightly beaten

⅓ cup butter, melted

1½ teaspoons salt

Ground cinnamon for sprinkling

1. In a large bowl, combine the water, yeast, and sugar. Mix well and let stand for 5 minutes, or until foamy. Stir in the milk and 2 cups of the flour and beat until smooth.

2. Beat in the eggs, butter, and salt and add enough flour to make a stiff, smooth dough (you may not need to add all of the flour).

3. Cover with a kitchen towel and let rise in a warm place until doubled in size, about 1 hour.

4. Generously butter a deep 2½-quart casserole or a 10-inch tube pan. Sprinkle the inside generously with cinnamon so the entire surface is dusted.

5. Stir down the batter and transfer to the casserole. Let rise in a warm place until the batter is within 1 inch of the top of the pan, about 45 minutes.

6. Meanwhile, preheat the oven to 350°F. Bake the bread for 45 minutes, or until a skewer inserted in the center of the loaf comes out clean and dry. Turn out of the casserole and serve hot.

MILK AND HONEY CASSEROLE BREAD

Honey brings out the nutty flavor of whole wheat in this bread. You will need 1 large or 2 smaller casseroles for this bread. A dish with straight sides, such as a soufflé dish, works best.

SERVES 12

- 1 cup milk
- ½ cup (1 stick) butter
- ½ cup honey
- 2 teaspoons salt
- 1 cup warm water (105 to 115°F)
- 2 packages (¼ ounce each) active dry yeast
- 1½ cups whole-wheat flour
- 4 cups bread flour or all-purpose flour

1. Pour the milk into a small saucepan and place over medium-high heat until scalded (about 200°F). Remove from the heat and add the butter, honey, and salt. Let stand until cooled to lukewarm and the butter is melted.

2. Meanwhile, in a large bowl, mix the warm water and dry yeast. Stir and let stand for 5 minutes, or until the yeast foams.

3. Stir the cooled milk mixture, whole-wheat flour, and 1 cup of the bread flour into the yeast mixture. With an electric mixer, beat at high speed for 2 minutes.

4. With a wooden spoon, beat in the remaining bread flour, a cupful at a time, and continue beating to make a sticky, soft dough. Cover with plastic wrap and let rise for 1 hour.

5. Coat one 3-quart casserole or two 1½-quart casseroles with cooking spray. Transfer the dough to the casserole(s) and let rise again for 1 hour.

6. Meanwhile, preheat the oven to 375°F. Bake the bread for 1 hour for the larger casserole or for 45 minutes for the smaller ones. Remove from the oven, turn out the loaves onto racks, and cool.

NO-KNEAD ARTISAN-STYLE CASSEROLE BREAD

The great flavor of this rather effortless bread comes from the long and slow rising period. When baked in a preheated casserole, it develops a nice crustiness. You will need a cast-iron Dutch oven or an enameled cast-iron pot (such as Le Creuset's) for baking the bread. This method was developed by Jim Lahey, the owner of the Sullivan Street Bakery in New York City, and reproduced by the food writer Mark Bittman in the *New York Times*. I found this method works well, but I have adapted it to my own favorite bread recipe.

SERVES 8 TO 10

2 cups tepid water (about 100°F)

1 teaspoon active dry yeast

2 teaspoons salt

4 to 4½ cups all-purpose flour

1. In a large bowl, stir the water and yeast together. Let stand for about 5 minutes, until the yeast is dissolved. Stir in the salt and 2 cups of the flour. Beat with a large spoon until smooth, then slowly add the remaining flour to make a rough, shaggy dough. It should look quite moist, but still hold together in a ball. Cover with plastic wrap and let rise at room temperature for at least 6 hours, or until the dough is dotted with bubbles.

2. Lightly flour a work surface and turn out the dough. Sprinkle with a little more flour and, using a dough scraper, lift the dough over onto itself to form a ball. Cover with a kitchen towel and let stand for 15 minutes.

3. Coat the kitchen towel generously with flour and place the ball of dough on top. Dust with more flour, cover with another kitchen towel, and allow to rise for about 2 hours, or until more than doubled in size.

4. Preheat the oven to 450°F. While the oven preheats, place a 4- to 5-quart heavy pot or Dutch oven into the oven, along with its lid, to preheat as well. This will take 20 to 30 minutes. When the dough is doubled and the pot is hot, place the pot on a board or trivet. Remove the towel covering the dough. Carefully slide your hand under the towel beneath the dough, pick up the towel and dough, and invert the loaf into the hot pot. Cover with the lid and bake for 30 minutes. Remove the lid and bake for another 15 to 30 minutes, until crusty. Turn out onto a rack to cool.

GOLDEN RAISIN AND WALNUT CASSEROLE BREAD

Cut thick slices of this bread and toast them for breakfast or coffee break. To make cinnamon toast, sprinkle the toasted and buttered bread with sugar and cinnamon.

SERVES 10

¼ cup warm water (105 to 115°F)

1 package (¼ ounce) active dry yeast

1 cup milk, scalded and cooled

¼ cup sugar

4 tablespoons butter, softened

1 teaspoon salt

2 large eggs, lightly beaten

1 cup golden raisins

2¾ to 3 cups all-purpose flour

1. In a large bowl, dissolve the yeast in the warm water. Let stand until foamy, about 5 minutes. Stir in the milk, sugar, butter, salt, eggs, and raisins.

2. Add the flour a little at a time, beating with an electric mixer until the dough is about the same consistency as cookie dough.

3. Cover with a kitchen towel and let stand in a warm place until doubled in bulk, about 1½ hours.

4. Butter a 2½- to 3-quart casserole. Stir the dough down and turn into the casserole. Cover and let rise until puffy, about 1 hour.

5. Meanwhile, preheat the oven to 350°F. Bake the bread for 25 to 30 minutes, or until a skewer inserted in the center of the loaf comes out clean and dry.

WHOLE-WHEAT RAISIN CASSEROLE BREAD

The combined flavors of honey, raisins, and whole wheat make this an all-time favorite for kids as well as adults.

SERVES 12

1 cup milk

½ cup (1 stick) butter

½ cup honey

2 teaspoons salt

1 cup warm water (105 to 115°F)

2 packages (¼ ounce each) active dry yeast

1½ cups whole-wheat flour

1 cup light or dark raisins

1 cup chopped walnuts

4 cups bread flour or all-purpose flour

1. Pour the milk into a small saucepan and place over medium-high heat until scalded (about 200°F). Remove from the heat and add the butter, honey, and salt. Let stand until the butter is melted and the mixture is cooled to lukewarm.

2. Meanwhile, in a large bowl, mix the warm water and dry yeast; stir and let stand for 5 minutes until the yeast foams.

3. Stir the cooled milk mixture, whole-wheat flour, raisins, walnuts, and 1 cup of the flour into the yeast mixture. With an electric mixer, beat at high speed for 2 minutes.

4. With a wooden spoon, beat in the remaining 3 cups flour, a cupful at a time, moistening all of the flour to make a sticky, soft dough. Cover with plastic wrap and let rise for 1 hour.

5. With cooking spray, coat one 3-quart casserole or two 1½-quart casseroles, preferably with straight sides. Put the dough in the casserole(s), cover with a kitchen towel, and let rise again for 1 hour until almost doubled.

6. Meanwhile, preheat the oven to 375°F. Bake the bread for 1 hour for the large casserole or 45 minutes for the smaller ones. Remove from the oven, turn the loaves out of baking pans, and cool on racks.

ROSEMARY AND PARMESAN CASSEROLE BREAD

Bake this in a shallow casserole, and you will end up with something that looks and tastes like classic focaccia!

SERVES 12

- 2 packages (¼ ounce each) active dry yeast
- ½ cup warm water (105 to 115°F)
- 1 cup creamed cottage cheese, warmed (see Note)
- 2 tablespoons sugar
- 2 tablespoons extra-virgin olive oil, divided, plus extra for the dish
- 2 teaspoons dried rosemary leaves, crushed
- 1 teaspoon salt
- 1 large egg
- 2 cups all-purpose flour
- 2 tablespoons grated Parmesan cheese

1. In a large bowl, dissolve the yeast in the warm water and set aside until foamy, about 5 minutes.

2. Add the warmed cottage cheese, sugar, 1 tablespoon of the olive oil, the rosemary, salt, and egg. Add the flour and beat well to make a stiff dough.

3. Cover with plastic wrap and let rise in a warm place for about 1 hour, or until doubled in bulk.

4. Brush a 9-by-13-inch shallow baking dish or pan with olive oil. Press the dough into the dish so it covers the bottom completely, including the corners. Cover with a kitchen towel and let rise in a warm place for about 1 hour, or until doubled in bulk.

5. Meanwhile, preheat the oven to 350°F. Drizzle the top of the dough with remaining 1 tablespoon olive oil and sprinkle with the grated Parmesan cheese. Bake for 30 to 35 minutes, until golden. Serve warm, cut into squares.

○○○○○

NOTE: To warm the cottage cheese, spoon into a glass 1-cup measure and microwave on high power for 30 seconds.

THREE-GRAIN CASSEROLE BREAD

You just stir up this dough, let it rise, and turn it into a casserole for baking. So simple! And it's so healthy, too, with all those grains.

SERVES 10

2 cups warm water (105 to 115°F)

2 packages (¼ ounce each) active dry yeast

3 tablespoons honey

1 cup nonfat dry milk

2 tablespoons butter, softened or melted

2 teaspoons salt

½ cup old-fashioned or quick-cooking rolled oats, plus extra for sprinkling

½ cup dark rye flour

1¼ cups whole-wheat flour

2½ cups unbleached all-purpose flour

1. Pour the warm water into a large bowl and stir in the yeast and honey until dissolved. Let stand until foamy, about 5 minutes.

2. Stir in the dry milk, butter, salt, the ½ cup oats, the rye flour, and whole-wheat flour and beat until smooth (you may do this with an electric mixer).

3. Slowly add the all-purpose flour, beating by hand or with the electric mixer (switching to a wooden spoon when the dough becomes too thick), until the dough resembles a thick cookie dough. Cover with a kitchen towel and let rise for 1 hour, or until doubled.

4. Generously butter a 2½- to 3-quart casserole and sprinkle the bottom and sides with rolled oats. Turn the batter into the casserole and sprinkle with more rolled oats. Let rise in a warm place until doubled in bulk, about 45 minutes.

5. Preheat the oven to 350°F. Bake the loaf for 45 minutes or until a skewer inserted in the center of the loaf comes out clean and dry. Remove from the oven and cool in the casserole on a rack for 10 minutes. Turn the bread out of the dish and finish cooling on the rack.

Chapter 4
BREAKFAST & BRUNCH CASSEROLES

Breakfast casseroles are perfect for entertaining early-morning guests. What's more, most of the recipes in this chapter can be assembled in the evening and baked in the morning, leaving time for other last-minute preparations if you are hosting a brunch.

Here are more than forty recipes. Most of them center on eggs and all that you can do with them, but there is one no-egg breakfast included, too. These recipes run the gamut from baked omelets, breakfast pies, ever-popular stratas, and hash-brown breakfasts to baked French toast, puffy baked pancakes, grits, polenta, and individual breakfast casseroles.

CONTINUED ON NEXT PAGE...

...CONTINUED

ARTICHOKE AND SALSA BREAKFAST CASSEROLE

For breakfast or brunch, a side of sliced fresh oranges, drizzled with a little balsamic vinegar, complements this egg-based casserole beautifully. Serve it with Cinnamon Bubble Bread (page 71).

SERVES 6

- 6 tablespoons tomato salsa (mild or medium)
- 1 can (14 ounces) artichokes, drained, rinsed, and chopped
- ¾ cup shredded sharp Cheddar cheese
- ¾ cup shredded Monterey Jack cheese
- 10 large eggs
- 1 cup light sour cream
- 6 tablespoons grated Parmesan cheese

1. Preheat the oven to 350°F. Coat 6 individual ovenproof dishes (6 to 8 ounces each) or one shallow 2-quart casserole with cooking spray.

2. Spread 1 tablespoon salsa in the bottom of each dish or all 6 tablespoons over the bottom of the large casserole dish. Spread the artichokes evenly over the salsa. Top with the shredded Cheddar and Monterey Jack cheeses (2 tablespoons each for the individual dishes).

3. Whisk the eggs and sour cream together, pour over the cheese in the dish(es), and top with the Parmesan. (At this point the dish(es) can be covered and refrigerated for up to 12 hours. Add 5 to 10 minutes to the baking time.)

4. Bake, uncovered, for 30 to 35 minutes or until set. Serve warm.

CHILE-WRAPPED CHEESE IN A BAKED PUFFY OMELET

The chile-wrapped Monterey Jack cheese gives this omelet a Southwestern flavor. Serve it as a simple main dish for lunch or brunch.

SERVES 6

½ pound Monterey Jack cheese

1 can (4 ounces) whole peeled green chiles

6 large eggs, separated

⅓ cup all-purpose flour

¾ teaspoon salt

1. Preheat the oven to 400°F. Butter a shallow 2-quart casserole or an 8-inch square baking dish.

2. Cut the cheese into strips ½ inch thick and 3 inches long. Remove and discard the seeds from the chiles. Cut each chile lengthwise into 3 strips. Wrap a chile strip around each piece of cheese; set aside.

3. In a large bowl, beat the egg whites with an electric beater until soft peaks form. Without washing the beaters, in a small bowl, beat the egg yolks until creamy. Beat in the flour and salt.

4. Fold the egg whites into the yolk mixture. Spread half of the egg mixture in the bottom of the buttered casserole. Top with the chile-wrapped cheese. Add the remaining egg mixture.

5. Bake, uncovered, for 15 to 20 minutes, or until set.

EGG AND MUSHROOM BAKED OMELET

This is so quick to put together, it could become a favorite breakfast when you have overnight guests.

SERVES 6

8 large eggs, beaten

½ pound mushrooms, sliced

½ cup chopped green onions (green and white parts)

4 slices bacon, cooked and diced, or ½ cup diced cooked ham

¼ pound shredded cheese, such as Cheddar, Swiss, or Jarlsberg

1. Preheat the oven to 350°F. Coat a shallow 1-quart shallow casserole with cooking spray.

2. In a large bowl, whisk together the eggs, mushrooms, green onions, bacon, and cheese. Pour the mixture into the dish and bake, uncovered, for 20 minutes, or until set. Cut into squares to serve.

SPANISH POTATO OMELET

In Spain this is called a potato tortilla, and it is often served in little squares on the tapas table. We think it is also a tasty breakfast dish. It's a great way to use leftover cooked potatoes.

SERVES 6

6 large eggs

2 cups peeled and cooked potatoes, cut into ½-inch dice

1 small onion, finely chopped

1 green pepper, minced

12 green stuffed Spanish olives, sliced

1 teaspoon salt

¼ pound cooked ham, cut into ½-inch cubes

1. Preheat the oven to 350°F. Coat a 9-inch round pie pan with cooking spray.

2. In a large bowl, beat the eggs until fluffy. Stir in the remaining ingredients and turn into the prepared pan.

3. Bake, uncovered, for 40 to 45 minutes, until the center is set. Cut into wedges to serve.

EGG CASSEROLE WITH CHILES AND COTTAGE CHEESE

This comes together in a flash! The butter melts in the baking pan in the oven while the oven preheats. Meanwhile, you quickly stir up the egg mixture. The green chiles and chili powder give this a Southwestern twist.

SERVES 8

4 tablespoons butter

10 large eggs

2 cups cottage cheese

1 pound Monterey Jack cheese, shredded

2 cans (4 ounces each) chopped green chiles

1 tablespoon chili powder

½ cup all-purpose flour

1 teaspoon baking powder

½ teaspoon salt

Sour cream for serving

Tomato salsa for serving

1. Preheat the oven to 350°F. Melt the butter in a 9-by-13 inch baking dish in the oven as it preheats. Remove the pan from the oven before the butter browns.

2. Beat the eggs until foamy. Mix in the cottage cheese, Monterey Jack cheese, chiles, chili powder, flour, baking powder, and salt.

3. Turn the mixture out into the dish with the melted butter and bake, uncovered, for 45 to 50 minutes, until the center is set. Let stand for 10 minutes before cutting. Serve with sour cream and salsa to spoon over individual servings.

EGGS FLORENTINE IN A CASSEROLE

This is reminiscent of an egg dish we enjoyed in New Orleans years ago at Brennan's Restaurant. It can be assembled ahead of time and refrigerated overnight.

SERVES 4

- 3 tablespoons butter at room temperature
- 1 package (10 ounces) chopped frozen spinach
- 3 tablespoons all-purpose flour
- 1½ cups milk, heated
- 4 large eggs, poached (see Note)
- 1 teaspoon salt
- ½ teaspoon pepper
- ½ cup grated Parmesan cheese or shredded mild Cheddar cheese

1. Preheat the oven to 400°F. Butter a shallow 1½-quart casserole with 1 tablespoon of the butter.

2. Cook the spinach according to package instructions and drain well.

3. In a small saucepan, over medium-high heat, melt the remaining 2 tablespoons butter. Blend in the flour and gradually whisk in the milk, stirring constantly, until thickened and bubbly.

4. Spread out the spinach in the prepared dish. Arrange the poached eggs over the spinach and pour the white sauce on top. Sprinkle with the salt, pepper, and cheese. (At this point the casserole can be covered and refrigerated. Add 10 minutes to the baking time.)

5. Bake, uncovered, for 3 to 5 minutes, or until the cheese is melted.

○○○○○

NOTE: To poach eggs, bring 2 inches of water to a simmer in a large skillet. Crack the eggs, one at a time, into a saucer. Slide the eggs, one at a time, into the simmering water. Baste the eggs with the boiling water and cook until done to your liking, about 3 minutes. With a spatula, lift the eggs from the water.

EGG, BACON, MUSHROOM, AND CHEESE CASSEROLE

This savory custard could be served for brunch or supper. Add a green or fresh fruit salad, freshly baked muffins, and hot coffee for a winning menu!

SERVES 6

- 1 tablespoon butter, plus extra for the dish
- 4 slices bacon
- 8 green onions, thinly sliced (white and green parts)
- 1 pound mushrooms, sliced
- 8 large eggs
- 1 cup milk
- 1 teaspoon salt
- ⅛ teaspoon pepper
- 2½ cups shredded Cheddar cheese

1. Preheat the oven to 350°F. Butter a shallow 2-quart casserole.

2. In a large skillet, cook the bacon until crisp; drain well and crumble. Add the green onions and the 1 tablespoon butter to the pan and cook for 2 minutes, stirring. Add the mushrooms and cook for 2 to 3 minutes more, then remove from the heat.

3. In a medium bowl, beat the eggs, milk, salt, and pepper together. Stir in the cheese and the mushroom mixture. Pour into the prepared dish and bake, uncovered, for 30 to 35 minutes, or until puffed and set.

BROCCOLI AND MUSHROOM FRITTATA

A frittata is a perfect way to use vegetables left over from last night's supper. Add them to the vegetables already in this colorful frittata. Make this tasty egg dish in just minutes for breakfast or for a brunch main dish.

SERVES 6

3 tablespoons butter

1 cup mushrooms, sliced

1 medium onion, chopped

½ medium red bell pepper, cut into 1-by-¼-inch strips

4 cups broccoli florets, blanched (see Note)

1 cup leftover cooked vegetables, such as peas, beans, or carrots (optional)

9 large eggs

1 teaspoon salt

1 cup shredded Cheddar cheese

1. Preheat the broiler. Melt the butter in an ovenproof, nonstick 10-inch skillet until sizzling. Add the mushrooms, onion, bell pepper strips, broccoli, and leftover vegetables, if using. Cook over medium heat until the mushrooms and onion are tender and the vegetables are hot, 3 to 4 minutes.

2. Beat the eggs and salt in a large bowl until frothy and pour into the skillet with the vegetables. Cook over medium heat, lifting slightly with a spatula to allow the uncooked portion to flow underneath, until the eggs are almost set, 3 to 4 minutes.

3. Sprinkle with cheese.

4. Broil about 8 inches from the heat until the cheese is melted and the eggs are set, 3 to 4 minutes.

NOTE: To blanch broccoli florets, bring a pot of water to a boil. Drop the florets into the water and cook for 1 to 2 minutes, until bright green.

NORWEGIAN BAKED CHEESE OMELET

Cheese is the backbone of the Scandinavian breakfast and brunch, and this omelet is made with nutty Norwegian Jarlsberg. It's really quick to make!

SERVES 4

4 large eggs

¼ cup water

½ teaspoon salt

2 tablespoons butter

¾ cup sliced green onions (white and green parts)

1 cup diced cooked ham

1 red bell pepper, seeded and cut into rings

¾ pound Jarlsberg cheese, cut into 1-inch cubes

Chopped parsley for garnish

1. Preheat the oven to 400°F.

2. In a medium bowl, whisk together the eggs, water, and salt. Melt the butter in a heavy flameproof shallow casserole or gratin dish over medium heat. Sauté the green onions, ham, and bell pepper for 3 to 4 minutes, until the green onions are bright green and the pepper is hot. Pour the egg mixture over them and sprinkle with the cheese cubes.

3. Bake, uncovered, for 15 to 20 minutes, until the egg mixture is set and the cheese is melted. Garnish with chopped parsley.

SAUSAGE, CHEESE, AND EGG CASSEROLE

This easy casserole is so quick to assemble, you can probably put it together while the oven preheats!

SERVES 8

12 large eggs, lightly beaten

⅓ cup all-purpose flour

½ teaspoon baking powder

10 ounces lean pork or turkey breakfast sausage, cooked and crumbled

2 cups shredded Monterey Jack cheese

1½ cups low-fat cottage cheese

½ pound mushrooms, sliced

1. Preheat the oven to 375°F. Butter a 9-by-13-inch glass baking dish.

2. In a large bowl, mix the eggs, flour, and baking powder. Stir in the sausage, shredded cheese, cottage cheese, and mushrooms.

3. Pour the mixture into the prepared baking dish and bake, uncovered, for 30 to 35 minutes, until set.

SOUTHWESTERN BREAKFAST CASSEROLE

I first had this spicy egg, cheese, and sausage casserole for breakfast in a wonderful inn in Santa Fe, New Mexico.

SERVES 8

6 ounces bulk-style chorizo sausage

½ onion, finely chopped

4 cans (4 ounces each) whole mild green chiles, drained

½ pound queso fresco (Mexican farmers' cheese), finely crumbled

8 large eggs, beaten

¼ teaspoon pepper

Tomato salsa for serving

1. Preheat the oven to 350°F. Butter an 8-inch square baking dish.

2. Place a medium skillet over medium-high heat. Add the chorizo and cook, breaking up with a fork, until browned, about 4 minutes. Add the onion and sauté for 3 to 4 minutes longer, stirring, until the onion is tender. Remove from the heat.

3. Cut each chile lengthwise in half and remove the membranes and seeds. Line the bottom of the dish with half the chiles, arranging them cut-sides up.

4. Sprinkle half of the chorizo mixture over the chiles and cover with half of the cheese.

5. Beat the eggs in a medium bowl and add the ground pepper. Cover the cheese layer with half of the beaten eggs. Top with the remaining chiles in one layer, and layer the remaining chorizo and then the cheese on top. Pour the remaining egg mixture over the cheese.

6. Bake, uncovered, for 30 to 40 minutes, until the casserole is set. Let stand for about 5 minutes before cutting into squares. Serve the squares topped with salsa.

SPINACH AND FETA BAKE

For a change in your evening routine, make this breakfast dish for supper.

SERVES 6

- 2 tablespoons butter, plus extra for the dish
- 1 medium red bell pepper, chopped
- 1 medium onion, chopped
- 3 cups baby spinach leaves
- ½ cup milk
- 8 large eggs
- ½ teaspoon salt
- ¼ teaspoon pepper
- ½ cup crumbled feta cheese
- 1 medium tomato, chopped, for garnish
- 1 tablespoon chopped fresh basil for garnish

1. Preheat the oven to 350°F. Butter a 9-inch pie pan.

2. In a medium skillet, melt the 2 tablespoons butter and add the bell pepper and onion. Cook over medium heat, stirring occasionally, until the vegetables are crisp-tender, 3 to 4 minutes. Add the spinach and continue cooking, stirring occasionally, until the spinach is wilted.

3. In a medium bowl, whisk together the milk, eggs, salt, and pepper. Stir in the cheese and the vegetable mixture. Pour into the pie pan.

4. Bake, uncovered, for 30 to 35 minutes, or until the eggs are set in the center and the edges are lightly browned. Let stand for 5 minutes. Garnish with the tomato and basil, cut into wedges, and serve.

SPINACH, HAM, AND EGG CASSEROLE

Serve this for brunch or as a side dish for dinner. Assemble it ahead of time and refrigerate it for up to 1 day, if you wish.

SERVES 6

- 2 tablespoons butter at room temperature
- 1 bag (1 pound) fresh baby spinach leaves
- 1 cup milk
- 3 tablespoons all-purpose flour
- 1 tablespoon dry mustard
- 1 teaspoon salt
- ½ cup shredded Cheddar cheese
- ½ pound deli ham, cut into ½-inch cubes
- 4 hard-cooked eggs, peeled and diced

1. Preheat the oven to 350°F. Grease a 1½-quart shallow casserole with a small amount of the butter.

2. Heat the remaining butter in a large skillet or wok over medium heat and add the spinach. Cook, stirring, until the spinach leaves are wilted. Add the spinach to the casserole.

3. In a saucepan, combine the milk, flour, mustard, and salt. Heat to boiling, whisking constantly. Cook for 3 minutes, stirring, until the mixture is thickened.

4. Sprinkle the spinach with the cheese and ham and pour the sauce over all. (At this point the casserole can be covered and refrigerated. Add 5 minutes to the baking time.)

5. Bake, uncovered, for 15 to 20 minutes, or until heated through. Remove from the oven and top with the hard-cooked eggs.

BREAKFAST EGG AND SUN-DRIED TOMATO PUFF

This dish puffs with the help of self-rising flour, which is popular in the South, but is not as readily available in the North. If you can't find it, you can make your own (see Note) or use Bisquick. Serve this with Cinnamon Sally Lunn (page 77) or toasted slices of Whole-Wheat Raisin Casserole Bread (page 81).

SERVES 8

- 2 tablespoons butter at room temperature
- 6 large eggs, beaten
- 2 cups milk
- 1 cup self-rising flour (see Note)
- 1 medium onion, chopped
- ½ cup finely chopped sun-dried tomatoes
- ½ cup chopped mushrooms
- 2 cups shredded Colby Jack or Cheddar cheese

1. Preheat the oven to 350°F. Coat a 9-by-13-inch baking dish with 1 tablespoon of the butter.

2. In a large bowl, whisk together the eggs, milk, and flour until smooth.

3. In a large nonstick skillet, melt the remaining 1 tablespoon butter over medium heat. Add the onion, sun-dried tomatoes, and mushrooms and sauté, stirring, until the onions are soft. Stir the vegetables into the egg mixture and mix in the cheese.

4. Pour into the prepared casserole. Bake, uncovered, for 35 to 40 minutes, until set. Serve hot.

○○○○○

NOTE: If you don't have self-rising flour on hand, add 1 teaspoon baking powder and ½ teaspoon salt to 1 cup all-purpose flour.

BREAKFAST POTATO PIE

This rather unusual dish is heaven for potato lovers! To keep the potatoes from turning brown after shredding, rinse in cold water and drain well.

SERVES 6 TO 8

2 tablespoons butter at room temperature

½ pound bacon, diced

¼ cup finely diced green bell pepper

¼ cup finely diced red bell pepper

1 small onion, chopped

8 large eggs

1 pound russet potatoes, peeled and shredded

2¾ cups shredded sharp Cheddar cheese

1 teaspoon salt

½ teaspoon pepper

1. Preheat the oven to 350°F. Coat a 10-inch pie or quiche dish with 1 tablespoon of the butter.

2. In a medium nonstick skillet, cook the bacon until crisp; remove the bacon and set aside. Drain all but 1 tablespoon of the bacon drippings. Add the peppers and onion and sauté over medium heat for 3 to 5 minutes, until soft.

3. Whisk the eggs in a large bowl. Stir the potatoes into the eggs. Add the bacon and the vegetable mixture. Pour into the prepared pan and spread out the mixture evenly. Top with the cheese and sprinkle with salt and pepper.

4. Bake for 45 minutes, or until set.

CRUSTLESS VEGGIE QUICHE

There is lots of flavor here from the garlic, vegetables, and herbs. The low-fat cheese makes it healthy, too.

SERVES 4

2 teaspoons butter, softened

1 large clove garlic, chopped

1 cup chopped broccoli

½ cup shredded carrot

2 green onions, sliced (white and green parts)

4 large eggs, beaten, or an equivalent amount of Egg Beaters

2 tablespoons water

½ teaspoon salt

1 tablespoon chopped fresh basil, or 1 teaspoon dried basil

½ cup shredded part-skim or regular Monterey Jack cheese

Sliced, seeded, and deribbed red bell pepper rings for garnish

1. Preheat the oven to 400°F. Grease a 9-inch pie pan with 1 teaspoon of the butter.

2. In a 10-inch nonstick skillet, melt the remaining 1 teaspoon butter and add the garlic, broccoli, carrot, and green onions. Cook over medium heat, stirring occasionally, until the vegetables are crisp-tender, 4 to 5 minutes. Spread over the bottom of the pie pan.

3. In a medium bowl, whisk the eggs, water, and salt together. Pour over the vegetable mixture and sprinkle with the basil.

4. Bake for 25 minutes or until set. Sprinkle the cheese over the top and garnish with the red pepper rings. Let stand until the cheese melts before serving.

CHEESE AND SAUSAGE BREAKFAST PIE

Here is a quichelike breakfast dish that's absolutely satisfying!

SERVES 8

1 recipe Flaky Pastry (page 32)

2 cups shredded mozzarella cheese

1 pound breakfast sausage, chopped, cooked, and drained

6 large eggs

½ cup milk

2 tablespoons snipped fresh chives

1. Prepare the pastry and chill in the refrigerator. Preheat the oven to 325°F.

2. Roll out the chilled pastry into a 12-inch circle and transfer to a 9-inch pie pan. Trim and crimp the edges.

3. Line the unbaked pie shell with 1 cup of the shredded cheese. Top with the sausage and the remaining cheese.

4. In a small bowl, beat the eggs and milk. Pour over the cheese layer evenly. Sprinkle with the chives.

5. Bake for 35 to 40 minutes, or until set.

CHICKEN AND ASPARAGUS BREAKFAST PIE

Similar to a quiche, this breakfast pie is perfect for a special brunch with friends or family. Start out with mimosas and add a freshly baked bread such as Whole-Wheat Bubble Bread (page 72).

SERVES 6 TO 8

FOR THE PASTRY:

1 cup all-purpose flour

¼ teaspoon salt

6 tablespoons chilled butter, cut into pieces

2 tablespoons chopped fresh chives

2 tablespoons cold water

FOR THE FILLING:

2 cups shredded Cheddar cheese

1 cup shredded cooked chicken

6 slices bacon, cooked until crisp and cut into 1-inch pieces

¼ pound asparagus

1½ cups half-and-half or milk

4 large eggs, lightly beaten

¼ teaspoon salt

⅛ teaspoon pepper

1. Preheat the oven to 400°F.

2. *To make the pastry:* In a food processor with the steel blade in place, combine the flour and salt; add the butter pieces. Process using on/off pulses about 8 times, until the mixture resembles coarse crumbs. Or, use a fork or pastry blender to cut the butter into the flour. Stir in the chives and then the water to make a crumbly dough. Shape into a ball.

3. On a lightly floured work surface, roll out the dough to make a 12-inch circle. Ease into a 10-inch pie pan, pressing the dough firmly against the bottom and sides. Crimp or flute the edges.

4. *To make the filling:* Spread the cheese over the bottom of the crust and top with the chicken. Sprinkle bacon over the chicken. Arrange the asparagus spears like the spokes of a wheel on top of the bacon.

5. Stir together the half-and-half, eggs, salt, and pepper in a medium bowl, and pour over the mixture in the pan. Bake for 40 to 45 minutes, or until golden and the center is set. Let stand for 10 minutes before serving.

HASH BROWN–CRUSTED POTATO PIE

Equally suitable for brunch or supper, this hearty breakfast pie only requires a side of fresh fruit or a salad for a satisfying meal.

SERVES 6

3 large eggs

½ cup milk

½ teaspoon salt

3 cups frozen shredded hash brown potatoes, thawed

5 tablespoons butter, melted

1 cup finely chopped cooked ham

1 cup shredded Cheddar or Swiss cheese

½ cup finely chopped onions

½ cup chopped green bell peppers

¼ cup diced red bell peppers

1. Preheat the oven to 425°F.

2. Mix the eggs, milk, and salt together in a medium bowl. Blot the potatoes between sheets of paper towels to remove excess moisture. Press the potatoes into the bottom and up the sides of an ungreased 9-inch pie pan. Drizzle with the melted butter.

3. Bake the crust for 25 minutes, or until lightly browned. Cool in the pan on a wire rack. Lower the oven heat to 375°F.

4. Spread the ham over the bottom of the crust. Top with the cheese, onions, and green and red bell peppers. Pour the egg and milk mixture over all.

5. Bake the pie for 35 to 40 minutes, or until set. Remove from the oven and let rest for 10 minutes before cutting and serving.

POTATO CRUST BREAKFAST PIE

We made 50 of these pies to feed 300 people for a brunch at church. When we compared the taste of a pie made with fresh tomatoes with one made with canned, the canned won out.

SERVES 6

FOR THE CRUST:

⅓ cup butter at room temperature, plus extra for the pan

¾ cup instant mashed potato flakes

¾ cup all-purpose flour

¼ cup grated Parmesan cheese

¼ teaspoon salt

¼ cup water

FOR THE FILLING:

1½ cups shredded Cheddar cheese

¼ cup instant mashed potato flakes

1 can (14½ ounce) diced tomatoes, drained

1 cup sliced mushrooms

FOR THE EGG MIXTURE:

5 large eggs

¼ cup sour cream

¾ teaspoon salt

1. Preheat the oven to 350°F. Butter a 9-inch pie pan.

2. *To prepare the crust:* In a medium bowl, stir the ⅓ cup butter, ¾ cup mashed potato flakes, the flour, Parmesan cheese, and ¼ teaspoon salt together until well mixed and crumbly. Drizzle the water over the dry ingredients and stir with a fork until the dough holds together.

3. Press the dough into the pie pan with your fingers and flute the edges. Bake for 10 minutes, or until the crust feels dry.

4. *To make the filling:* Spread ½ cup of the shredded cheese, the ¼ cup mashed potato flakes, tomatoes, and mushrooms evenly over the top. Top with the remaining 1 cup cheese.

5. *To make the egg mixture:* Beat together the eggs, sour cream, and ¾ teaspoon salt. Carefully pour over the ingredients in the pie shell, poking a hole here and there to allow the mixture to permeate the filling.

6. Bake for 25 to 30 minutes, until a knife inserted in the center comes out clean and the filling is set. Cool for about 10 minutes before cutting and serving.

BAKED CINNAMON-MAPLE FRENCH TOAST

Remember this simple dish when you have houseguests. Put it together the night before and refrigerate it, covered. It's perfect for a leisurely winter morning. Your guests will wake up to the great smells of cinnamon and maple as the French toast bakes.

SERVES 8

- 1 loaf 2-day-old French bread, cut into 1-inch-thick slices
- 12 large eggs
- 2 tablespoons pure maple syrup
- 1 quart heavy cream
- 1½ tablespoons vanilla extract
- Cinnamon for garnish
- Butter at room temperature, for serving
- Warmed maple syrup for serving

1. Put the bread slices in a 9-by-13-inch baking dish.

2. In a large bowl, whisk together the eggs, maple syrup, heavy cream, and vanilla. Pour over the bread and let set for 1 hour. Turn the slices, cover, and refrigerate overnight.

3. In the morning, turn the bread once again and sprinkle with cinnamon. Let stand for 15 minutes before baking.

4. Preheat the oven to 350°F. Bake the French toast, uncovered, for 40 to 45 minutes, until the toast feels firm to the touch and no egg mixture appears around the edges. Serve with butter and warmed maple syrup.

BAKED COCONUT FRENCH TOAST WITH TROPICAL FRUIT COMPOTE

This is definitely a summery brunch dish. When strawberries are in season, add them to the compote as well.

SERVES 8

FOR THE COMPOTE:

1½ cups chopped pineapple

1 cup chopped mango

1 cup chopped papaya

1 cup chopped kiwifruit

3 tablespoons sugar

3 tablespoons fresh lime juice

FOR THE FRENCH TOAST:

16 slices French bread (1 inch thick), cut on the diagonal

1¼ cups light coconut milk

6 large eggs, lightly beaten

½ cup sugar

1 tablespoon vanilla extract

½ cup sweetened flaked coconut

1. *To prepare the compote:* Combine the pineapple, mango, papaya, kiwifruit, sugar, and lime juice in a serving bowl. Cover and chill for 8 hours or overnight.

2. *To make the French toast:* Coat a 9-by-13-inch baking dish with cooking spray. Arrange the bread in a single layer in the bottom. Combine the coconut milk, eggs, sugar, and vanilla, stirring with a whisk. Pour evenly over the bread, and turn the bread over to coat. Cover and refrigerate for 8 hours or overnight.

3. Preheat the oven to 350°F.

4. Remove the bread mixture from the refrigerator and uncover. Turn the bread slices over, and sprinkle evenly with the flaked coconut. Let stand at room temperature for 15 minutes. Bake, uncovered, for 30 minutes, or until the coconut is golden. Serve warm with the fruit compote.

BAKED FRENCH TOAST WITH PRALINE AND MAPLE SYRUP

You might serve this with sliced fresh strawberries when they are in season. In winter, serve with sliced bananas and oranges on the side.

SERVES 6 TO 8

1 cup (2 sticks) butter, plus extra for the dish

One loaf (1 pound) French bread

8 large eggs

2 cups half-and-half

1 cup milk

2 tablespoons granulated sugar

½ teaspoon salt, or more to taste

1 teaspoon vanilla extract

1 teaspoon ground cinnamon, divided

½ teaspoon ground nutmeg, divided

1 cup packed light brown sugar

1 cup chopped pecans

2 tablespoons light corn syrup

Maple syrup for serving

1. Butter a 9-by-13-inch baking dish. Cut the bread into 20 slices, about 1 inch thick. Arrange the slices in the baking dish in 2 rows, overlapping the slices.

2. In a large bowl, combine the eggs, half-and-half, milk, sugar, salt, vanilla, ½ teaspoon of the cinnamon, and ¼ teaspoon of the nutmeg. Beat with a rotary beater or whisk until blended but not bubbly.

3. Pour the mixture over the bread slices, making sure all are covered evenly with the milk and egg mixture. Spoon some of the mixture in between the slices. Cover with foil and refrigerate overnight. Remove from the refrigerator 15 minutes before baking.

4. Preheat the oven to 350°F.

5. For the praline topping, in a medium bowl, combine the 1 cup butter, the brown sugar, pecans, corn syrup, the remaining ½ teaspoon cinnamon, and the remaining ¼ teaspoon nutmeg. Spread the praline mixture evenly over the bread. Bake for 35 to 40 minutes, until puffed and lightly browned and the center of the casserole is set. Serve with maple syrup.

BAKED PECAN-STUFFED FRENCH TOAST

Pumpkin pie spice—a combination of cinnamon, ginger, allspice, and cloves—has a special affinity for egg and milk mixtures. This is a perfect choice for a holiday breakfast or brunch.

SERVES 8

1 cup firmly packed light or dark brown sugar

½ cup (1 stick) butter

2 tablespoons honey

1 cup chopped pecans, toasted (see Note)

1 large loaf (1 pound) French bread, cut into ½-inch-thick slices

½ pound cooked ham, finely chopped (2 cups)

6 large eggs, beaten

1⅔ cups milk

1 teaspoon vanilla extract

1 tablespoon sugar

1 teaspoon pumpkin pie spice (see Note)

Maple syrup for serving

1. Combine the brown sugar, butter, and honey in a small saucepan. Cook over medium heat, stirring frequently, until the butter melts and the sugar dissolves, 2 to 3 minutes. Pour into an ungreased 9-by-13-inch baking dish. Sprinkle with the pecans. Top with half of the bread slices, and scatter the ham on top.

2. Combine the eggs, milk, and vanilla in a large bowl and beat until well mixed. Dip the remaining bread slices in the egg mixture on one side only. Place over the ham, dipped side down. Pour the remaining egg mixture over the bread slices. Combine the sugar and pumpkin pie spice in a small bowl and sprinkle over the top. Cover the baking dish and refrigerate for 4 hours or overnight. Remove from the refrigerator 15 minutes before baking.

3. Preheat the oven to 350°F.

4. Uncover the French toast and bake for 50 to 55 minutes, or until golden brown and a knife inserted in the center comes out clean. Let stand for 10 minutes. Cut into 8 servings. Serve with maple syrup.

○○○○○

NOTES: If you don't have pumpkin pie spice, substitute ½ teaspoon ground cinnamon, ¼ teaspoon ground ginger, ⅛ teaspoon ground nutmeg, and ⅛ teaspoon ground cloves.

To toast the pecans, preheat the oven to 350°F. Spread out the nuts on a cookie sheet and bake, stirring occasionally, for 5 to 10 minutes, until aromatic and lightly browned.

BLUEBERRY-MAPLE FRENCH TOAST WITH BLUEBERRY SAUCE

You definitely want to use fresh blueberries with this one. When I made it with frozen blueberries, the blueberry juice turned the French bread and custard a sickly shade of purple while baking. The flavor was still delicious, however, and our granddaughter just about devoured the whole thing!

SERVES 8

1 large loaf (1 pound) French bread, crust removed

1 package (8 ounces) cream cheese

1 cup fresh blueberries

12 large eggs, beaten

2 cups milk

⅓ cup maple syrup

FOR THE BLUEBERRY SAUCE:

1 cup sugar

1 cup water

2 tablespoons cornstarch

1 tablespoon butter

1 cup blueberries

1. Cut the bread into 1-inch cubes and spread half in a 9-by-13-inch baking dish. Cut the cream cheese into cubes and scatter over the bread. Scatter the blueberries evenly on top and cover with the remaining half of the bread cubes.

2. Mix the eggs, milk, and maple syrup in a large bowl and pour over the bread mixture. Cover and refrigerate overnight. Remove from the refrigerator 30 minutes before baking.

3. Preheat the oven to 350°F. Cover the dish with aluminum foil and bake the French toast for 30 minutes. Uncover and bake for 30 minutes longer, until set.

4. *While the French toast bakes, make the blueberry sauce:* Combine the sugar, water, cornstarch, and butter in a medium saucepan. Place over medium heat and boil for 3 minutes, stirring constantly. Stir in the blueberries, reduce the heat, and simmer for 8 to 10 minutes, until the blueberries burst.

5. Slice the French toast and serve warm with the warm blueberry sauce.

CINNAMON AND APPLE–STUFFED FRENCH TOAST CASSEROLE

Here's another idea for breakfast or brunch. It's a very flexible recipe. Assemble the casserole a day ahead if you like, or just before baking. For other fruit flavors, check the variations below.

SERVES 4

- 4 large slices sourdough bread, crust removed, and cubed
- 1 package (8 ounces) cream cheese, cubed
- 1 large Golden Delicious or Granny Smith apple, peeled and chopped
- 6 large eggs
- 1 cup milk
- 1½ teaspoons ground cinnamon
- 3 tablespoons powdered sugar for garnish

1. Preheat the oven to 375°F. Arrange half the bread cubes in an 8-inch square baking dish. Distribute the cream cheese cubes evenly over the bread. Distribute the chopped apple over the top, and cover with the remaining bread cubes.

2. Beat the eggs, milk, and cinnamon together in a medium bowl and pour over all. Bake for 35 minutes, uncovered. Sprinkle with powdered sugar before serving.

Variations

Fresh Blueberry–Stuffed French Toast Casserole: Substitute 2 cups blueberries for the apple and proceed with the recipe.

Fresh Strawberry–Stuffed French Toast Casserole: Substitute 2 cups sliced strawberries for the apple and proceed with the recipe.

Toasted Almond and Peach–Stuffed French Toast: Replace the apples with 2 large peaches, peeled and sliced. Scatter the peaches over the cream cheese cubes, sprinkle with ½ cup toasted slivered almonds, and proceed with the recipe.

HAM AND CHEESE–STUFFED FRENCH TOAST

I served this to a group of my husband's friends who get together once a year. It was a real favorite. For a lunch or supper dish, serve it with sauerkraut on the side.

SERVES 8

½ cup (1 stick) butter at room temperature, divided, plus extra for the dish

12 to 14 slices rye bread with caraway seeds

3 tablespoons Dijon-style mustard

1 sweet onion, thinly sliced

¾ pound Asiago, Swiss, or Cheddar cheese, thinly sliced or shredded

¾ pound thinly sliced cooked ham

6 large eggs

2½ cups milk

1 tablespoon chopped fresh basil, or 1 teaspoon dried basil

1 teaspoon salt

1½ cups fine dry breadcrumbs or panko (see Note)

¼ cup grated Parmesan cheese

1. Butter a 9-by-13-inch baking dish. Using 3 tablespoons of butter, lightly butter all of the bread slices on one side. Spread the mustard on top. Arrange half of the bread slices, mustard side up, in the baking pan in one layer; cut to fit if necessary.

2. Heat 1 tablespoon of the remaining butter in a skillet over medium-low heat and add the onion. Sauté for 25 to 35 minutes, stirring often, until the onion is softened. Spread the onion evenly over the bread slices. Top with half the sliced cheese and all of the ham. Cover with the remaining cheese and then the remaining bread slices. Press the layers together.

3. Beat the eggs, milk, basil, and salt together in a medium bowl. Pour evenly over the layers, pressing them down slightly so they absorb the mixture. Cover and refrigerate for several hours or overnight. Remove from the refrigerator 1 hour before baking.

4. Preheat the oven to 375°F. Mix the breadcrumbs with the remaining 4 tablespoons butter and the Parmesan cheese in a medium bowl. Sprinkle over the casserole. Bake, uncovered, for 35 to 40 minutes, until the top is golden brown and the egg mixture is set. Remove from the oven and allow to rest for 10 minutes before serving. To serve, cut into squares.

○○○○○

NOTE: Panko are Japanese-style coarse breadcrumbs, which stay crisp longer than regular dried breadcrumbs.

HOT PEPPER STRATA

The "hot" comes easily with a sprinkle of red pepper flakes, but be sure to add them according to your taste!

SERVES 8

10 slices whole-wheat bread

2 cups sliced mushrooms

1 cup sliced green onions (white and green parts)

1 can (4 ounces) diced green chiles

3 cups shredded sharp Cheddar cheese

6 large eggs

2 cups milk

1 tablespoon Dijon mustard

1 to 3 teaspoons red pepper flakes

1 cup crushed tortilla chips

1. Butter a 9-by-13-inch baking dish.

2. Remove the crusts from the bread and put the crusts (not the bread) into a food processor fitted with the steel blade. Process to make crumbs and set aside until you're ready to bake the strata.

3. Line the baking dish with half the bread slices in one layer, cutting them to fit if necessary. Top with half the mushrooms, half the green onions, half the green chiles, and half the cheese. Cover with the remaining bread slices, mushrooms, green onions, chiles, and cheese.

4. Whisk together the eggs, milk, mustard, and red pepper flakes in a medium bowl. Pour over the ingredients in the dish. Cover and refrigerate for 4 hours or overnight. Remove from the refrigerator 30 minutes before baking.

5. Preheat the oven to 350°F. Mix the reserved breadcrumbs with the tortilla chips and sprinkle over the top of the casserole. Bake, uncovered, or 55 minutes, or until set. Let stand for 10 minutes before serving.

MUSHROOM-STUFFED CROISSANT CASSEROLE

Make this with day-old croissants. This is another savory dish that is assembled the night before.

SERVES 4

- 1 tablespoon butter, plus extra for the dish
- 4 plain croissants, split horizontally
- 2 cups sliced mushrooms
- ¼ cup sliced green onions (white and green parts)
- 4 large eggs
- 1 cup milk
- 1 cup shredded Swiss cheese
- 1 cup shredded mozzarella cheese
- ¼ cup grated Parmesan cheese

1. Butter a 9-inch square casserole. Arrange the croissant bottoms, cut sides up, in the bottom of the dish.

2. Melt the 1 tablespoon butter in a skillet and add the mushrooms and green onions. Sauté over medium heat, stirring, for 2 to 3 minutes, until the liquid is evaporated. Remove from the heat.

3. Whisk the eggs and milk together in a small bowl and pour half of the mixture over the croissants. Top with the mushroom mixture. Top with the cheeses, then pour the remaining liquid over the top.

4. Position the croissant tops, cut side down, over the bottoms, with the filling mixture in between. Cover and refrigerate overnight. Remove from the refrigerator 30 minutes before baking.

5. Preheat the oven to 350°F.

6. Bake the casserole for 35 to 40 minutes, or until set. Let stand 10 minutes before serving.

ONION AND GOAT CHEESE BREAD PUDDING

Have it for breakfast, brunch, or supper—this meatless main dish is delicious any time. Serve it with a refreshing salad of some kind, one with fresh fruit or marinated vegetables.

SERVES 6 TO 8

5 tablespoons butter at room temperature, plus extra for the dish

1 loaf (1 pound) sourdough bread, sliced, crusts removed, and cut into ¾-inch cubes

3 bunches green onions, cut into ½-inch lengths (white and green parts)

1 large clove garlic, finely chopped

½ teaspoon salt

Dash of cayenne pepper

4 large eggs

1½ cups heavy cream

¾ cup sour cream

1 tablespoon chopped fresh basil, plus extra for garnish

1 log (10½ ounces) goat cheese, crumbled

1. Preheat the oven to 400°F. Butter a 9-by-13-inch baking dish.

2. Spread out the bread cubes on an ungreased baking sheet and toast for 10 minutes, turning them often, and making sure they don't burn.

3. In a large skillet, melt the 5 tablespoons butter and add the green onions and garlic. Sauté over medium-high heat for 3 minutes, or until the green onions are aromatic. Add the salt and cayenne pepper.

4. Whisk the eggs, cream, and sour cream together in a large bowl. Add the sautéed green onions, the 1 tablespoon basil, and the crumbled cheese. Fold in the toasted bread cubes and turn into the prepared baking dish. Cover and refrigerate overnight. Remove from the refrigerator at least 30 minutes before baking.

5. Preheat the oven to 350°F. Bake, covered with aluminum foil, for 25 minutes. Uncover and bake for another 20 minutes, or until the top is browned, the edges are bubbly, and the center is cooked. Sprinkle with additional chopped basil.

SAUSAGE AND CHEDDAR EGG DISH

Make-ahead breakfast casseroles are really convenient, and this is one of our favorites.

SERVES 6 TO 8

6 large eggs

1 cup half-and-half

2 tablespoons green onions, chopped (white and green parts)

1 teaspoon salt

½ teaspoon pepper

1 tablespoon butter at room temperature

6 slices Texas toast or another thick-cut, crusty white bread

1 pound spicy pork sausage, cooked and drained

1 cup grated Cheddar cheese

1. In a medium bowl, beat the eggs. Add the half-and-half and green onions. Mix well, season with the salt and pepper, and set aside.

2. Spread the butter over the bottom and sides of a 9-by-13-inch baking dish. Line the dish with the bread, cutting and rearranging, if needed. Sprinkle the bread with the cooked sausage and the cheese. Pour the egg mixture over all. Cover and refrigerate overnight. Remove from the refrigerator 30 minutes before baking.

3. Preheat the oven to 350°F. Uncover the dish and bake for 35 to 40 minutes, or until the casserole is set in the center. Let stand 5 to 10 minutes before cutting into serving pieces.

BELL PEPPER AND SAUSAGE STRATA

I bake a lot of French bread, and often some of the loaf goes uneaten. I cut these hunks into cubes, crusts and all, and freeze them. Here's how I use them!

SERVES 6

- 1 package (12 ounces) frozen pork breakfast sausage, thawed and crumbled
- ⅓ cup chopped green bell pepper
- ⅓ cup chopped red bell pepper
- 6 cups day-old French bread cubes (¾-inch cubes)
- 1½ cups half-and-half or undiluted evaporated milk
- 4 tablespoons butter, melted
- 3 large eggs
- 1 teaspoon onion salt
- 1½ cups shredded Cheddar cheese

1. In a heavy skillet over medium heat, cook the sausage and green and red peppers for about 4 minutes, until the sausage is browned and the peppers are crisp-tender. Drain off the fat if necessary.

2. In a large bowl, combine the cooked mixture with the bread cubes and turn into an ungreased 8-inch square baking dish or a shallow 2-quart casserole.

3. Combine the half-and-half, butter, eggs, and onion salt. Pour evenly over the bread mixture in the pan. Sprinkle the cheese evenly on top. Cover tightly and refrigerate overnight. Remove from the refrigerator 30 minutes before baking.

4. Preheat the oven to 350°F. Uncover the strata and bake for 55 to 60 minutes, or until a knife inserted in the center comes out clean and the cheese is melted. Let stand for 5 minutes before serving.

TURKEY SAUSAGE, EGG, AND CHEDDAR BAKE

Low-fat turkey breakfast sausage comes in frozen logs, available in the freezer section of your market, and sometimes in bulk packages, sold at the meat counter. A variety of breads, from rye to wheat, are perfect in this breakfast dish. I like to save ends of bread, cut them into cubes, and store in zip-top bags in the freezer. When I have about 5 cups, I put this casserole together.

SERVES 6

- 1 pound bulk turkey breakfast sausage
- 6 slices assorted day-old bread, cubed
- 1 cup shredded Cheddar cheese
- 6 large eggs
- 2 cups milk
- 1 teaspoon salt
- 1 teaspoon dry mustard
- ⅛ teaspoon cayenne pepper

1. Butter a 9-by-13-inch baking dish. In a skillet, crumble and cook the sausage over moderate heat until browned. Drain well.

2. Spread half of the bread cubes in the baking dish. Top with half of the cheese and all of the sausage. Cover the sausage with the remaining bread cubes and the remaining cheese.

3. Mix the eggs, milk, salt, dry mustard, and cayenne pepper in a large bowl. Pour this mixture over the ingredients in the dish. Cover and refrigerate for at least 12 hours. Remove from the refrigerator 30 minutes before baking.

4. Preheat the oven to 350°F. Uncover the dish and bake for 1 to 1½ hours, or until set (baking time will vary, depending on how cold the ingredients are).

THREE-CHEESE BREAKFAST CASSEROLE

Manchego is Spain's most famous cheese. It was made originally from the milk of Manchego sheep, which grazed on the famous plain of La Mancha. Sometimes, when I have just a dried heel of the cheese left, I combine it with other cheeses I have on hand and transform its marvelous flavor into a breakfast casserole.

SERVES 6

6 tablespoons butter at room temperature

6 slices thick-cut bread, crusts trimmed

½ teaspoon pepper

½ cup shredded Swiss cheese

½ cup shredded sharp Cheddar cheese

½ cup shredded Manchego cheese

1½ cups whole milk

6 large eggs

2 teaspoons fresh oregano leaves, or ½ teaspoon dried oregano

1. Butter 6 individual 8-ounce ramekins or one 9-inch square baking dish using 1 tablespoon of the butter.

2. With the remaining 5 tablespoons butter, spread one side of each slice of bread with butter. Place a single slice, buttered side up, in each ramekin, or lay the buttered slices in the baking dish. Grind some pepper over each slice of bread.

3. Mix the three types of cheese together. Sprinkle each bread slice in a ramekin with ¼ cup of the cheese mixture, or sprinkle all of the cheese over the bread in the baking dish. Beat the milk with the eggs in a medium bowl and add the oregano. Pour over the cheese and bread in the ramekins or baking dish. Cover and refrigerate overnight.

4. The next morning, preheat the oven to 350°F. Remove the casserole(s) from the refrigerator 30 minutes before baking and uncover.

5. Bake the ramekins for 20 to 25 minutes or the larger dish for 35 to 40 minutes, until puffed and golden brown. Serve immediately.

EGGS BENEDICT CASSEROLE

With this safe method of cooking eggs for hollandaise sauce, we can once again enjoy this classic dish without worry. The casserole method allows you to do most of the preparation ahead of time and serve with ease.

SERVES 6

12 slices toasted white or wheat bread, crusts removed

12 slices Canadian bacon

12 cold large eggs

FOR THE HOLLANDAISE SAUCE:

6 large egg yolks

½ cup water

¼ cup fresh lemon juice

1 cup (2 sticks) cold butter, each stick cut into eighths

¼ teaspoon salt

¼ teaspoon paprika

Chopped fresh parsley for garnish

1. Preheat the oven to 250°F. Butter a 9-by-13-inch baking dish. Place the toast pieces side by side in the baking dish and top each with Canadian bacon.

2. Poach the eggs in 3 batches: In a deep skillet, bring 2 to 3 inches of water to a boil. Reduce the heat and maintain the water at a gentle simmer. Break 4 cold eggs into a bowl. Holding the bowl close to the water's surface, slip the eggs into the water. Cook until the whites are completely set and the yolks begin to thicken but are not hard, about 3 to 5 minutes. With a slotted spoon, lift out the eggs and place them, one at a time, onto the bacon-topped toasts. Repeat with the remaining eggs. (At this point the casserole can be covered and refrigerated overnight. Take out of the refrigerator 15 minutes before baking.)

3. *To make the hollandaise sauce:* In a small saucepan, beat together the egg yolks, water, and lemon juice. Cook over very low heat, stirring constantly, until the mixture bubbles at the edges.

4. Whisk in the butter, 1 piece at a time, and continue whisking until all the butter is melted and the sauce is thickened. Stir in the salt and paprika. Remove from the heat and cover and chill if not using immediately. (To reheat, transfer to the top of a double boiler or a bowl suspended over a saucepan of simmering water and whisk briskly until the sauce is smooth and pourable.)

5. To finish the casserole, drizzle hollandaise sauce over the poached eggs. Bake for 15 minutes, or until heated through. Garnish with the chopped fresh parsley.

BAKED GRITS WITH CHEESE

Easy and filling, this falls into the "comfort foods" category—perfect for breakfast, brunch, or a light supper.

SERVES 6

- 2 tablespoons butter, plus extra for the dish
- 4 cups water
- 1 teaspoon salt
- 1 cup cornmeal grits or polenta
- 1 large egg
- ⅓ cup heavy cream
- 1 teaspoon pepper
- 1 cup grated Gruyère cheese
- ⅓ cup grated Parmesan cheese

1. Preheat the oven to 350°F. Butter a 2-quart casserole.

2. In a medium saucepan, heat the water and salt to boiling. Gradually whisk in the grits and cook, whisking constantly, until thickened, about 15 minutes.

3. Whisk the egg, cream, the 2 tablespoons butter, and pepper together in a small bowl. Stir into the cooked grits along with the Gruyère and Parmesan cheese. Transfer to the casserole.

4. Bake, uncovered, for about 45 minutes, until set. Remove from the oven and let sit for about 5 minutes before serving.

GRITS, CHEESE, AND EGG BREAKFAST CASSEROLE WITH TOMATO SALSA

Put this hearty casserole on the menu for a Tex-Mex brunch or lunch. Serve with a simple bean dish, along with the fresh salsa.

SERVES 6

4 tablespoons butter, melted, plus extra for the dish

4 cups water

2 teaspoons salt

1 cup cornmeal grits

6 large eggs, beaten

1 tablespoon onion, finely chopped

1 cup milk

½ cup yellow cornmeal

2 tablespoons all-purpose flour

1 teaspoon baking powder

1 pound bulk pork sausage, cooked and drained

2 cups shredded Monterey Jack cheese

½ teaspoon paprika

Roasted Tomato Salsa (recipe follows) for serving

1. Preheat the oven to 350°F. Butter a 9-by-13-inch baking dish or baking pan.

2. Bring the water and 1 teaspoon salt to a boil in a large deep saucepan over high heat. Gradually add the grits, reduce the heat to medium, and cook, stirring often, until thick, about 30 minutes. Set aside to cool slightly.

3. In a large bowl, mix the eggs, onion, remaining 1 teaspoon salt, the milk, cornmeal, flour, baking powder, and the 4 tablespoons butter. Stir in the cooked grits.

4. Spread the cooked pork sausage evenly over the bottom of the casserole and spread the cornmeal mixture on top. Spread the cheese over the top and sprinkle evenly with paprika. (The casserole can be assembled ahead of time up to this point, covered, and refrigerated overnight. Remove from the refrigerator 30 minutes before baking.)

5. Bake, uncovered, for 45 to 50 minutes, or until firm in the center. Let stand for 5 minutes before serving. Accompany with Roasted Tomato Salsa.

ROASTED TOMATO SALSA

MAKES ABOUT 2 CUPS

6 Roma (plum) tomatoes, quartered lengthwise, then halved crosswise

1 red onion, cut into 1-inch dice

1 jalapeño pepper, seeded and cut into eighths

2 tablespoons olive oil

Juice from ½ lime

Salt and pepper

½ cup chopped fresh cilantro

1. Preheat the oven to 450°F. Line the inside of a shallow baking pan with foil and coat with cooking spray.

2. In a large bowl, toss the tomatoes, onion, and pepper with the olive oil and spread out in the pan. Roast for 10 minutes and let cool in the pan.

3. Transfer the mixture to a medium serving bowl and season with the lime juice, salt and pepper to taste, and cilantro.

GRITS AND EGGS

These grits are baked with eggs and cheese to make one of the most basic of grits casseroles, and a very satisfying one at that.

SERVES 6

- 4 cups water
- 1 teaspoon salt
- 1 cup cornmeal grits
- 3 large eggs, separated
- 2 teaspoons baking powder
- ½ cup shredded sharp Cheddar cheese

1. Preheat the oven to 325°F. Butter a shallow 2-quart casserole.

2. In a large deep saucepan over high heat, bring the water and salt to boiling and stir in the grits. Lower the heat to medium and cook, stirring often, for 30 minutes, or until thick. Set aside for a few minutes to cool slightly.

3. Beat the egg yolks in a small bowl. Stir in a small amount of the grits to temper them, then stir the yolks into the pan full of grits.

4. Beat the egg whites until stiff with an electric mixer, and fold into the grits mixture. Fold in the baking powder and cheese. Transfer to the casserole and bake, uncovered, for 35 to 40 minutes, until slightly browned and puffy. Serve immediately.

POLENTA, CHEESE, AND EGG CASSEROLE

You can make this casserole ahead of time, cover, and refrigerate, and do the baking just before serving.

SERVES 6

- 6 cups water
- 1½ cups polenta or coarse yellow cornmeal
- 1 pound Cheddar cheese, shredded
- 3 large eggs, beaten
- 3 teaspoons seasoning salt
- 2 pounds bulk sausage, crumbled, cooked and drained
- 1 teaspoon paprika

1. Preheat the oven to 350°F. Butter a deep 3-quart casserole.

2. In a large saucepan, bring the water to a boil and slowly whisk in the polenta. Cook, stirring, over high heat until thickened. Lower the heat and stir in the cheese.

3. Stir a small amount of the cooked polenta into the beaten eggs to temper them, then stir the egg mixture into the polenta in the saucepan along with the salt, cooked sausage, and paprika. Pour into the casserole and bake, uncovered, for 1½ hours, or until set.

MUSHROOM AND POTATO BREAKFAST CASSEROLE

The low-fat dairy products bring the total fat content down (despite the bacon) to make a healthier breakfast casserole. If you serve this for brunch, add a baby spinach salad with sliced fresh strawberries when in season, and dress with a simple vinaigrette with a bit of honey added.

SERVES 4

4 slices white or whole-wheat bread, crusts removed

6 large eggs

1½ cups skim or low-fat milk

4 slices bacon, cooked and crumbled

¼ cup shredded reduced-fat Cheddar cheese, divided

¼ cup shredded reduced-fat Swiss cheese, divided

⅓ cup sliced mushrooms

½ cup frozen shredded hash brown potatoes, thawed

1. Coat an 8- or 9-inch square baking dish with cooking spray and arrange the bread slices across the bottom, overlapping them slightly.

2. In a large bowl, beat the eggs, milk, bacon, 2 tablespoons of the Cheddar cheese, 2 tablespoons of the Swiss cheese, and the mushrooms. Pour the mixture over the bread slices and sprinkle with the potatoes, then sprinkle with the remaining cheese. Cover and refrigerate overnight. Remove 30 minutes before baking.

3. Preheat the oven to 350°F. Bake, uncovered, for 40 to 45 minutes, or until lightly browned and the eggs are set.

HASH BROWN BREAKFAST CASSEROLE

This is one of those casseroles that you can make ahead or not—whatever best suits your schedule. Frozen hash brown potatoes save time here without compromising taste.

SERVES 6

- 1 pound bacon
- 2 tablespoons butter
- 2 onions, chopped
- 2 cups sliced mushrooms
- 4 cups frozen shredded hash brown potatoes, thawed
- 1 teaspoon salt
- ½ teaspoon pepper
- 6 large eggs
- 1½ cups milk
- 2 tablespoons chopped fresh parsley
- 1 cup shredded mild to sharp Cheddar cheese

1. Preheat the oven to 400°F. Separate the bacon slices and arrange on a large rimmed baking sheet. Place in the oven as it preheats and bake until the bacon is crisp, 10 to 12 minutes. Drain off the fat.

2. Using 1 tablespoon of butter, coat a shallow 3-quart casserole.

3. Melt the remaining tablespoon of butter in a nonstick skillet. Add the onions and mushrooms and sauté over medium heat, stirring, for 5 to 10 minutes, until the onions are tender.

4. Arrange the potatoes in the bottom of the dish, and sprinkle with the salt and pepper. Top with the cooked bacon slices, then the onions and mushrooms.

5. In a large bowl, beat the eggs with the milk and parsley. Pour over the casserole and top with the cheese. (The casserole can be assembled up to this point, covered, and refrigerated. Add 15 minutes to the baking time.)

6. Bake the casserole, uncovered, for 45 minutes, or until set and the cheese is melted. Serve immediately.

LUMBERJACK HASH BROWNS, EGG, AND CHEESE CASSEROLE

As its name suggests, this casserole is perfect for a day of skiing, snowshoeing, or just snow shoveling, thanks to its substantial stick-to-the-ribs quality.

SERVES 6

4 tablespoons butter, plus extra for the dish

12 large eggs

1 cup plain regular or nonfat yogurt

1 teaspoon salt

¼ cup chopped sweet onions

2 cups shredded fresh potatoes, preferably russets

1 cup shredded sharp Cheddar cheese

1. Preheat the oven to 350°F. Butter a 9-by-13-inch glass baking dish.

2. In a large bowl, beat the eggs, yogurt, and salt together.

3. In a medium skillet over medium-high heat, melt the 4 tablespoons butter and add the onions and potatoes. Sauté for 3 to 4 minutes, until the vegetables are beginning to soften.

4. Add the onion-potato mixture to the egg mixture and transfer to the prepared casserole. Bake, uncovered, for 30 to 35 minutes, or until a knife inserted in the center of the mixture comes out clean. Top with the cheese, cut into 6 generous portions, and serve.

NO-EGG BREAKFAST POTATO HOT DISH

Add this dish to a brunch menu just for variety. It is also a great way to use leftover cooked potatoes.

SERVES 6

2 teaspoons butter

1 small onion, minced

4 cups diced cooked potatoes

8 slices bacon, cooked and crumbled

1 cup shredded Cheddar or Swiss cheese

¼ cup sliced pimiento-stuffed green olives

½ cup light mayonnaise

1. Preheat the oven to 350°F. Coat an 8-inch square baking dish with cooking spray.

2. Melt the butter in a nonstick skillet, and cook the onion over medium-high heat until tender, about 5 minutes.

3. Transfer the onion to a large bowl and add the potatoes, cooked bacon, cheese, olives, and mayonnaise, stirring until well mixed. Transfer to the prepared baking dish. Bake, uncovered, for 30 to 35 minutes, until lightly browned and bubbly around the edges. Serve immediately.

POTATO-CRUSTED HAM AND CHEESE BAKE

Hash browns form a hearty crust for this easy brunch or lunch dish. This is lovely with a fresh fruit salad and hot muffins.

SERVES 6

2 cups frozen shredded hash brown potatoes, thawed

1 cup light cream or half-and-half

4 large eggs

¼ teaspoon pepper

1 cup cubed cooked ham (½-inch cubes)

¼ cup finely sliced green onions (white and green parts), divided

¼ cup finely chopped red bell pepper, divided

1 cup shredded medium or sharp Cheddar cheese, divided

1. Preheat the oven to 375°F. Coat a 9-inch pie pan with cooking spray and press the potatoes onto the bottom and up the sides of the pan. Bake for 10 minutes.

2. Combine the cream, eggs, and pepper in a medium bowl and beat until well mixed. Stir in the ham, 2 tablespoons of the green onions, and 2 tablespoons of the red pepper. Sprinkle half of the cheese over the potatoes. Pour the egg mixture over the cheese.

3. Bake, uncovered, for 35 to 40 minutes, or until a knife inserted in the center comes out clean. Top with the remaining cheese, 2 tablespoons green onions, and 2 tablespoons red pepper. Let stand for 10 minutes before serving.

SAGE, POTATO, BACON, AND CHEESE CASSEROLE

When sage is growing in my garden, I often make this breakfast casserole. It's a also a good recipe to make when you have some leftover potatoes.

SERVES 8

1 pound sliced bacon, diced

1 medium sweet onion, chopped

8 large eggs, lightly beaten

4 cups diced cooked potatoes

2 cups shredded mild Cheddar cheese

1½ cups small-curd cottage cheese

1¼ cups shredded Swiss cheese

2 tablespoons chopped fresh sage leaves, or 1 tablespoon dried

1. Preheat the oven to 350°F. Butter a 9-by-13-inch glass baking dish.

2. Spread out the bacon and onion on a rimmed baking sheet and bake until the bacon is browned and crisp, about 10 minutes. Drain.

3. Transfer the bacon and onion to a large bowl and stir in the eggs, potatoes, cheeses, and sage. Transfer to the prepared baking dish. Bake, uncovered, for 25 to 30 minutes, or until the eggs are set. Let stand for 10 minutes before serving.

HERB-BAKED CHEESE AND EGG CASSEROLE

You can multiply the quantities in the ingredients list to accommodate any number of guests. This is really a per-serving recipe. Bake it in individual custard cups or 4- to 6-ounce ramekins.

SERVES 1

1 tablespoon butter, melted

1 large egg

1 tablespoon half-and-half

1 tablespoon shredded mild Cheddar cheese

Pinch of dried basil

Pinch of dried oregano

Pinch of dried thyme

Pinch of dried parsley

Pinch of pepper

2 teaspoons grated Parmesan cheese

Dash of paprika

1. Preheat the oven to 350°F. Pour the butter into an individual ovenproof casserole or ramekin. Top with the egg. Spoon the half-and-half over the top and sprinkle with the Cheddar cheese, the herbs, pepper, Parmesan, and paprika.

2. Place in a larger baking dish and add 1 inch of boiling water to the larger dish. Bake for 20 minutes, or until the egg is set. When done, run a knife around the edge and drain off any extra liquid.

PUFFY OVEN APPLE PANCAKE

Large and puffy baked pancakes are popular throughout Europe; I was first introduced to this recipe in Finland. The proportion of eggs, milk, and flour varies from one recipe to another, but this is my favorite. It puffs up to make a golden, crusty cradle. I like to fill it with fruit or berries at the table. Cook the sautéed apple slices while the pancake bakes and bring them to the table in a serving bowl. A 17-inch slope-sided paella pan is perfect for baking the pancake.

SERVES 4

FOR THE PANCAKE:

1½ cups all-purpose flour

1½ cups milk

6 large eggs

1 tablespoon sugar

1 teaspoon salt

½ cup (1 stick) butter

FOR THE APPLE FILLING:

2 large Golden Delicious or Granny Smith Apples, peeled and sliced

2 tablespoons butter

¼ cup light or dark brown sugar

Whipped cream for serving (optional)

1. *To make the pancake:* In a bowl, whisk together the flour, milk, eggs, sugar, and salt until no lumps remain. Let stand for 30 minutes. (You can mix the batter the night before, cover, and refrigerate. Remove from the refrigerator when you begin preheating the oven.)

2. Preheat the oven to 450°F. While the oven preheats, place a large slope-sided baking pan or ovenproof skillet into the oven and add the butter. When the butter is melted, remove from the oven.

3. Pour the pancake mixture into the heated pan and return to the oven. Bake the pancake for 15 to 20 minutes, until the edges are puffed high and golden.

4. *To make the apple filling:* While the pancake bakes, in a medium skillet, sauté the apples in the butter until tender, 5 to 10 minutes. Add the brown sugar and stir until dissolved. Transfer to a serving bowl.

5. To serve the pancake, be sure guests are at the table when you bring it in, as it will slump quickly. Cut the pancake into quarters, and fill each serving with sautéed apples. Pass whipped cream on the side, if desired.

SWEDISH LINGONBERRY PANCAKE CASSEROLE

Many people enjoy their Swedish pancakes, which are as thin as crêpes, with lingonberry preserves. Here's a way to make the pancakes ahead of time and reheat them in casserole form so that you, the cook, will be able to enjoy the fruits of your labor. This makes a pretty presentation when you unmold the casserole onto a serving plate. Cut into wedges to serve.

SERVES 6

3 tablespoons butter, melted, plus extra for the dish

½ cup sugar

1 tablespoon cinnamon

3 large eggs

2½ cups milk

1¼ cups flour

½ teaspoon salt

Vegetable oil for cooking the pancakes

1 jar (14 ounces) lingonberry preserves, plus extra for serving (optional)

Whipped cream for serving

1. Preheat the oven to 325°F. Butter an 8-inch round casserole or soufflé dish. Stir the sugar and cinnamon together in a small bowl.

2. In a large bowl, beat the eggs with half the milk. Add the flour and salt and stir until smooth. Stir in the 3 tablespoons melted butter and the remaining milk; the batter will be thin.

3. Heat a griddle or large nonstick skillet with about 1 tablespoon of vegetable oil. For each pancake, pour about ¼ cup batter onto the griddle and cook over medium heat for about 1 minute, until the pancake develops golden brown spots on the bottom side. With a spatula, turn the pancake and cook until golden brown, about 30 seconds. Continue cooking the pancakes, adding more oil to the pan as needed. You will end up with about 15 or 16 thin pancakes, about 8 inches in diameter.

4. Place each pancake into the prepared casserole as it is cooked. Sprinkle each with cinnamon sugar and spread with lingonberry preserves and layer them in the casserole dish. (At this point the casserole can be covered and refrigerated for serving later.)

5. Before serving, bake, uncovered, for 15 minutes or until heated through. Cut into wedges and serve with whipped cream and additional lingonberry preserves, if desired.

THREE CHEESES AND CHILE CUSTARD

This baked custard makes a tasty breakfast, but it can also be cut into small squares and served with crisp tortilla chips as a snack or appetizer. To make this casserole even quicker and easier, purchase already shredded cheeses.

SERVES 6

4 large eggs

½ teaspoon baking powder

¼ cup whole-wheat flour

½ teaspoon dry mustard

1 cup cottage cheese

1 cup shredded Cheddar cheese

1 cup shredded Monterey Jack cheese

2 cans (4 ounces each) chopped green chiles

Sliced avocado for garnish

Tomato salsa (mild, medium, or hot) for garnish

1. Preheat the oven to 350°F. Coat a 2-quart shallow casserole with cooking spray.

2. In a large bowl, beat the eggs. Add the baking powder, flour, and mustard and stir until smooth. Stir in the cheeses and chiles. Pour into the casserole and bake, uncovered, for 25 to 30 minutes, until set.

3. To serve, cut into squares and garnish with slices of avocado and dollops of salsa.

Chapter 5

POULTRY CASSEROLES

Chicken offers such a variety of choices, it can be mind-boggling: cook it whole, cut it into pieces, leave the bone in and skin on or not. No wonder it is a favorite with adults and children alike.

The bland flavor of chicken makes it easily adaptable to many cuisines. Flavored with curry and coconut milk, it becomes a Vietnamese dish (page 158). Made with ginger, garlic, and chiles and served over basmati rice, it is transformed into an Indian-inspired biryani (page 157).

What's more, chicken is high in protein but relatively low in fat, particularly the breast. Chicken breast becomes dry if overcooked, however, so it is a perfect candidate for casseroles. Enjoy classics such as Country Captain Casserole (page 152), French coq au vin in a casserole (page 184), King Ranch Chicken (page 170), and Chicken Marengo (page 178), Napoleon's favorite.

The casseroles in this chapter use various types of chicken meat: boneless breasts; bone-in breasts; whole chicken, cut up; just legs or thighs; and cooked chicken meat. There are also some recipes made with turkey and duck.